ISBN 978-1-330-43189-4
PIBN 10050568

1 MONTH OF
FREE
READING

at

www.ForgottenBooks.com

By purchasing this book you are eligible for one month membership to ForgottenBooks.com, giving you unlimited access to our entire collection of over 1,000,000 titles via our web site and mobile apps.

To claim your free month visit: www.forgottenbooks.com/free50568

Hurrah! hurrah! for England,
  Till woods and valleys ring,
Hurrah! for good old England,
  Hurrah for England's King.

Strong ships are on her waters;
  Firm friends upon her shores;
Peace, peace within her borders,
  And plenty in her store.

Right joyously we are singing,—
  We are glad to make it known
That we love the land we live in,
  And our King upon the throne.

Then hurrah! for merry England;
  And may we daily sing
The triumphs of our country
  And praises of our King.

CANADIAN GRAMMAR.

What language is spoken in the Dominion of Canada? Canadian.

Do you mean the English language? Yes.

Then, why not always call it the English language? Because in England there are different kinds (or dialects) of English. We choose one, and may, if we prefer, call it Canadian.

Do you know that Shakespeare and Milton and others wrote good English, and that we ought to follow them, and moreover call our language English? No. No. These writers by example might recommend a system of imparting thought, but no one is supposed to imitate them, no more than the writers of other languages, unless indeed he chooses so to do.

What is the object of this book? The object is to teach how the English language is spoken and written in Canada.

Are we bound to know the history of the language? No. That has nothing to do with the usuages of to-day. Many words have lost their old meaning, and all we have to do is to learn how to employ them in their present senses, and practise the same.

PREFACE.

My Dear Children, and Ladies and Gentlemen:

Here is a new Grammar, which I believe you will like.

It is not intended for our good scholars who would possibly teach myself; but is written for the youth who with dictionary and other helps are trying to master or mistress the English language.

I believe this book will benefit students of the different Grades from Grade 3 up to Grade 11. Other books on Grammar may be used with advantage. In no case will the price of this book exceed twenty:five cents, therefore, it may be expected that many who are learning Grammar will have a copy.

The Cape Breton Giant, which I published in 1899, A D. was much praised. For this and for buying so readily, I thank you now. I needed money then and many bought and so got me beyond trouble. I must mention some particular patrons:—

Duncan McDonald, Glendyer, Mabou.
John D. McIsaac, Port Hood.
Alex. A. Gillis, Mira.
Literary Society Cape Breton County,
      (which includes C. J. Bruce, Mr. Stewart and
      other scholars of eminence) Cape Breton County.
Mrs. Allan MacLellan, Port Hood.
Mrs. Jno. P. Murphy, Glace Bay.
Allan MacDonald, Barrister, Sydney.
W. P. Fraser, New Glasgow.
Mrs. Alex. R. MacLellan, Broad Cove Church.
Jno. MacKinnon, Inspector of Schools, Whycocomagh.
Donald E. MacLean, Teacher, Inverness.
Mary Bell MacDonnell, Judique.
A. C. Bertram, North Sydney.
Mr. Finlayson, a teacher of Whycocomagh high school—
      a native of Pictou.
Catherine A. MacDonald, Teacher, Victoria County.
Joseph R. Murphy, Emerald, Margaree.
Peter Gillis, River Warden, S. W. Port Hood—a perfect
      man.

I ought to add a tribute to our great Inspector of Schools.
A high scholar, an orator, a worker, an honest man and a friend
he is in a remarkable degree. His predecessor, Jno. G. Gunn,
was an extraordinary man. He took Grade A early in his day,
and his inspectoral career knew no blemish. On retiring from
failing health, great was our sorrow; and had Mr. MacKinnon
been not amiable and able, the change would be keenly felt,
if not resisted. By the way, Mr. Gunn was preceded by James
MacDonnell whose son is Registrar of Deeds at Port Hood.
Reverting to Mr. MacKinnon he always cheers me in literary
work, calling me in fun, "our only author."

I tremble when I think of thanking our Superintendent
of Education, A. H. MacKay, for all he has done for me. He
is as easily approached in business, as a child, and like the
folks "in the big house," is good to everybody.

I would like to touch a string in praise of His Lordship
Bishop Cameron, Rev. A. Chisholm, Judique, and Rev. Mr.
MacDonald, Strathlorne. The former's knowledge of language
is prodigious.

I shall now give the names of other people whom I have
in one manner or another found helpful:—

The late Hugh Gillis, Warden, Upper Margaree, one of
the finest men that ever lived. He died in 1903.
He was born at East Bay in 1817, and was married
to good Margaret MacDonnell.

Alexander H. Gillis,   Upper Margaree.
Malcolm H. Gillis, Teacher.   "
James A. McFarlane, Teacher.   "
Jno. D. MacLellan, Merchant.   "
Alex. MacLellan, Teacher.
Ronald MacDonnell (Archd.)   "
Allan A. Cameron.
James E. Gillis, Montana
Duncan Gillis, Turner.
Catie Ann MacFarlane.
Jno. Grant MacFarlane.
Annie MacFarlane.
Simon Gillis, (Angus), S. W. Margaree
James M. MacDonald, S. W. Margaree.   A fine scholar.
Mrs. John A. MacDougall, B. C. Banks.
A. L. MacDougall,   S. W. Margaree.
Angus Collins & Co.   "
Catherine Ann MacEachen.   "

Michael Gillis, Teacher, Broad Cove.
Margaret Ann MacLellan, Deepdale.
Neil L. MacIsaac, Judique.
Jno. Archd. MacDonnell, Judique Intervale.
Lauchlin MacDonald, Judique Ponds.
Angus J. MacDonald,   "
Angus A. MacDonnell, Judique Church.
Malcolm MacEachen,   Judique
Alex. MacDonnell (Hugh)   "
Flora MacDonald.   "
Mrs. Hugh MacDougall.
John P. MacDougall.
Guarrie MacQuarrie, Teacher,   Lake Ainslie
John C. MacInnes, Teacher   "
Murdoch MaLean, Dalhousie student.   "
Michael MacCormick, Rome student.   "

I think this book will do much good.   That it will is the
sincere wish of the author, and I hope no one will have reason
to regret making for its sake an outlay of twenty-five cents.

I am, yours truly,

JAMES D. GILLIS,

Teacher.

EASY GRAMMAR.

ETYMOLOGY.

FUNCTION.

The function of the eye is to see. The function of the ear is to hear. The functions of the tongue are two, namely, to taste and to speak. In like manner, the words we use in talking have different functions. Only for this, one word would be enough in any language.

GRAMMAR.

Only lawyers know very much of the law of the land, but every man knows enough of the law to know right from wrong. Every person knows the chief or principal laws. Now, grammar is a collection of the principal laws of language. There are many laws of language, a great many. The mastering of them all would take years. Many of these laws are not essential. The collection of laws which we call grammar are by far the most useful.

Grammar treats of the classification of words according to their functions, and of the different forms words take to perform different functions. Grammar, moreover, treats of the order, or arrangement, of words in sentences.

The object of grammar being twofold, namely, first to tell the different forms of words in different cases, and second, the order of words in our statements, it is divided into two grand? parts, Etymology and Syntax.

The object of the classification is merely to enable us to apply the laws of Etymology and Syntax. The knowledge of classification is of no value in itself.

ETYMOLOGY.

Etymology gives and defines the sets, or classes, into which it is necessary to divide the words of our statements, or sentences, in order to learn to apply the laws of grammar. Etymology, also, tells of the different forms of words, in different cases, or circumstances. In the statement, Me give those book to he yesterday's, it is not hard to see that something is wrong. It is not etymological. Now the laws of Etomology would teach this way:—I gave that book to him yesterday.

CLASSIFICATION.

Before giving the classes of words, the term sentence may be defined. A sentence is anything said, or written, to make another, or others, know one or more of our thoughts, as, The good lady played the piano sweetly.

Now, in the course of the day, the functions that we desire words to perform for us are properly eleven. Therefore, there are first eleven classes of words, and called parts of speech. They are the Noun, Adjective, Pronoun, Verb, Adverb, Preposition, Conjunction, Interjection, Infinitive, Participle and Gerund. Again, sometimes we find that we often employ more than one word to perform the function of one word. On this account there are two more parts of speech, the Compound and the Post-Compound.

THE PARTS OF SPEECH DEFINED. .

A Noun is the name of a thing which we can see, feel, etc., as horse, and also of a thing which we can only fancy, as death, mind, etc.

Exercise—Point out the Nouns.

The horse hauls wood. The ship has a large cargo. James played on the flute. Water is plentiful. My mind to me a kingdom is. Pleasures are like poppies spread. The length of that river exceeds my expectations. Your beauty pleases me.

THE ADJECTIVE.

An Adjective is a word used for the purpose of description as pretty, tall, and red, in the following sentences:—I saw pretty flower. The tall man walks briskly. Give me that red apple.

Adjectives are employed, also, to suggest or express a limit to a number or quantity of things spoken about. Adjectives are moreover employed instead of pointing with the hand, as this, these, that, those. These, however, are but Limiting Adjectives. In the following sentences the words three, several, few and many are Limiting Adjectives:—I saw three birds. Several boys returned. A few men are working. Many girls succeed.

Exercise—Point out the Adjectives.

Give me a good apple. I saw a fast horse. Several boys saw the comet. A few ladies have arrived. You are a better writer than you were. I want the best boat. Little baby lay your head on your pretty cradle bed.

THE PRONOUN.

Pro. means for. Pronoun means for a Noun. So a Pronoun is a word used instead of a Noun. In the following sentences the words I, she, him, who, few, many and brave are Pronouns:—I am going to see him. She is well. Few, few, shall part where many meet. The combat deepens, on ye brave. I saw the man who told you.

Exercise—Point out the Pronouns.

He is talking to them. I shall do what I desire. How sleep the brave? We saw one another before. Who are you? Whoever told you that made a mistake. I saw himself yesterday.

THE VERB.

A Verb is any word that asserts action, or tells us of inaction, as if it were action.

In the following sentences ran, walked, sawed, asserts action:—James ran fast. Cassie walked slowly. Bob sawed a board.

In the following sentences the words rest, sleep, die, express inaction as if it were action, that is they suggest action:—The boys rest. The children sleep. They die.

THE ADVERB.

An Adverb is a word used to tell how, why, when or where an action was actually performed, or supposed to be performed.

Adverbs are also often used in description of state. For instance, He is **asleep**. I was **driving**. And Adverbs sometimes limit the sense of Adjectives, and also of other Adverbs. For instance, I saw an **extremely** rich man. She sang **very sweetly**.

Adverbs ending in ing are called Active Adverbs. In the sentence, I was driving, driving is an Adverb Active, of manner.

In the following sentences the words well and swiftly tell how actions were actually performed:—Joseph worked well. John ran swiftly.

In the following sentences the words soundly and well tell how a supposed action (so to speak) was performed:— John sleeps soundly. The baby rests well.

Exercise—Point out the Adverbs.

I came yesterday. I came here. I came home. I walked briskly. I laughed heartily. John wrote fast. The bird flew about. Just above the falls I saw a bird. I arrived early. I went to work.

THE PREPOSITION.

A Preposition is a word used to tell the relationship of place between a verb and some object.

In the following sentences the words under, below, and on are Prepositions:—The boy is under the tree. He went under the bridge. I saw a man below the falls. He walks on the bridge.

THE CONJUNCTION.

A Conjunction is a word that suggests union of objects, of actions, or of states. As, John and James are well. John worked and sang. John sleeps and dies. In the foregoing sentences, and is a Conjunction.

In the following sentences, but, or, for, and, although, are Conjunctions:—John went, but Harry stayed. You may go or stay. I liked him, for he was worthy. He stayed, although I did not insist upon him.

The main object of Conjunctions is brevity, as, He went, He returned, is shortened by a Conjunction into, He went, but returned.

THE INTERJECTION.

An Interjection is a word employed specially to announce sorrow, wonder, joy, etc.

In a manner, the Interjection is not a separate part of speech, but a distillation of the other seven parts of speech into "one burning drop," for the Interjection, Oh! tells more sometimes than the longest winding sentence could.

THE INFINITIVE.

The Infinitive is a word which performs two functions, that of a Noun, and that of a Verb.

We must not suppose it to be partly Noun and partly Verb, but a perfect and complete Noun, and a perfect and complete Verb.

In the following sentences the words do and gone are Infinitives:—You know the way to do it. I have gone. In the second sentence, have denotes the possession (so to speak) of the performing of a deed, or action, just completed. It has, therefore, the same meaning as have in the sentence, I have a book.

THE GERUND.

A Gerund differs but little in form and sense with the Infinitive. The Gerund ends in ing, and denotes action going on. At the same time, it is the name of something.

In the following sentences, dancing, and walking are Gerunds:—He is fond of dancing. Walking is healthful.

The Gerund derived from Affecting Verbs may take an object, as By singing songs, he lives.

THE PARTICIPLE.

The Participle is a part of speech that is a full Verb and a full Adjective.

As Verbs, Participles have two Tenses, the Present and the Past, as loving, driven. Yet, bear in mind, we cannot know it by appearance. Care may be taken in knowing them from Active Adverbs and from Infinitives. The man driving is wise—driving is a Participle. The man is driving—driving is an Active Adverb. The untilled land is barren—untilled is a Participle. I have tilled it—tilled is an Infinitive

THE COMPOUND.

The Compound is a part of speech made up of several words properly used but making no statement.

The fifth, sixth and seventh words of the following sentence constitute a Compound:—He took the gun to protect himself.

THE POST COMPOUND.

The Post Compound is a group of words that makes a statement, but a statement that leans, or depends, upon some other statement.

ANALYSIS.

Grammatical Analysis is the separating of a sentence into parts according to the functions which the parts perform.

Every sentence is possible of division into two grand parts, namely, Subject and Predicate. In many cases the Subject is made up of parts, and so is the Predicate.

The Subject may consist of the real Subject, the Enlarge: mend and the Complement.

The Predicate may consist of the real Predicate, the Extension, the Object, the Enlargement of the Object, and the Objective Complement.

In Analysis we may find two Objects in a sentence, the Indirect and the Direct. The Indirect comes before the Direct.

Verbs of urging, making, etc., may seem to take a second Object, but it is better to consider the second Object an Adverb. Study—I made him swift. I made him leave. I made him King. Here, King is plainly an Adverb of Degree. They deemed him penurious. Penuriously deemed is he. Penurious is an Adverb of Manner.

EXAMPLE OF A PARSING TABLE.

The child might first study the exact function of each word.   MOTTO:—Leave old customs to the old.—

JAMES D. GILLIS, Teacher.

Word	Class	Sub-Class	Forms	Relation	Rule of Etymology or Syntax or both.
You	Pron	First Person	Common Gender, Either Numb., Nom.	Subj. of may	The subj. precedes the Verb. The subj. is Nom.
May	Verb	Unaffecting, W. Conj. Parts—may, might, might	No Voice, Declarative Mood, Present Tense	Agrees with you with regard to Number	A Finite Verb agrees, etc.
Go	Adv.	Manner		Modifying may	Adv. modify, etc.

Note.—Is he free? Yes. To what extent? He may go. Go, then, is the limit. We may suppose he is not allowed to do anything else. Go, is an Adverb, setting limits to the state suggested by may.

Word	Class	Sub-Class	Forms	Relation	Rule of Etymology or Syntax or both.
John	Noun	Individual	Msc., Sing., Nom.	Subj. of wrote	The subj. precedes, etc. The subj. is Nom.
Wrote	Vrb	Affecting	Active, Decl hée, Past Person, Sing. Third	Agrees with John in Number	The Verb agrees, etc.
A	Adj.	Limiting		Limiting letter to show that no special l tter is meant.	Adj. limit Nouns.
lter	Nun	Gal	N uter Gender, Sing. ive	Object of wrote	Affecting Verbs take the Objective.

PARSING.

Parsing is finer Analysis. Parsing is the naming of a word, (etc. in a sentence) a Noun, or Pronoun, etc., according to its function. In Parsing we give further information about the particular form of the word used, its relation to other words and we usually justify a part of this work by quoting a rule. In Parsing sentences containing Compounds, and Post Compounds, besides naming these parts of speech, we give further information about their particular sense in each case, and finally parse its words, or parts.

The object of the practice of Parsing is to quicken our minds in applying the laws of grammar in making sentences of our own.

"Memory is generally understood to be an intellectual faculty. Our dictionaries define the word as, "that faculty of the mind by which it retains and can recall previous ideas and impressions," and indeed the word is rarely, if ever, used with any other meaning than that implied in this definition.

Yet if we consider a little, it must be apparent that all memory does not belong to consciousness. There is the unconscious as well as the conscious memory. Consciousness is little concerned with those numerous bodily movements, which we daily execute with such ease. The intellect of the skilled musician does not guide—or even follow—his fingers in the execution of a piece of music. The mind knows little of those complex movements which take place in walking, running or dancing. Still less in speaking has the intellect to remember how to adjust each little fibre and muscle in order to produce a desired word. That which makes possible all these complex and varied movements, is the memorty of the muscles and of the *motor nerves*. Memory is not confined to consciousness; the whole nervous system remembers.

But the memory of the *motor nerves*—or, as it has been very appropriately called by some psychologists, *motor memory* —differs from the *intellectual* or *phsycical* memory in some very marked respects. For instance, a juggler who has practised a series of movements, would be unable to perform them in a different order to that in which he has practised them, nor could he commence anywhere in the series and continue them on. Let him be disturbed but for one moment while performing let him miss but one link in his chain of movements, and he is obliged to begin again at some point further back. .

It is not necessary, however, to have seen a juggler performing, in order to understand the peculiarities of *motor* memory just referred to. All who have heard the amateur at the piano, know that his playing consists chiefly in stopping short and beginning over again. Each one's personal experience, too, will furnish him with other examples which will fully illustrate this point.

But *motor* memory, though in one sense distinct from *psychical* memory, yet is so associated and related to the latter, that we are liable to confound the two. A poem, when learned for the first time, is learned by means of *psychical* memory. The meaning of the words—the thoughts or ideas which they represent—is seized hold of by the mind and retained by it. By constantly reciting the poem, however, the words become, as it were, incarnate in us. The nervous elements which bring about the movements resulting in speech, become so modified by the repetition of the lines, that we not only remember the ideas in the poem, but we preserve in our very nervous system a copy—if I may so call it—of the words, in the order in which we have been repeating them. When, therefore, the poem shall have been *intellectually* forgotten—that is to say, when all the ideas, which we had gathered from it, shall have passed from our mind—the *motor* elements, in moments of restlessness will place upon our lips the words of the poem, while all the time our intellect may be occupied with some widely different matter.

Now, whether it be a poem we unconsciously recite, or a series of remembered movements, we unconsciously go through with the fingers, or limbs, in either case, the movements will be performed in the fixed order in which they have been practised. Never without the interference of the intellect do we recite a line backwards which has not been learned in that way. Words, when learned in rotation, or succession, are remembered as ordinary barren movements. If any one word is the series be left out, we require to begin anew in order to remember what follows. As in humming an air, a false note may put us all astray. Those who have never learned to recite the letters of the alphabet backwards can only do so by an utmost effort of the attention.

We see, then, that *motor* memory has its disadvantages. It is true that it is more stable, and more persistent, than *psychical* memory. It is rare that one forgets how to swim or how to skate after he has once learned. A poem thoroughly learned by heart is learned forever; and indeed the most meaningless rhymes or combinations of words are often the most perfectly remembered. Nevertheless *motor* memory should never be substituted for *psychical* memory, when ideas, not mere movements, are to be remembered. For intellectual impressions, though tending to fade more quickly than *motor* impressions, are not like the latter, chained together in any fixed order. An *idea* has a thousand different roads by which it may usher itself into consciousness.

Nearly every one is familiar with the rhyme, "Thirty days hath September," etc., yet how many of those who depend on this rhyme can tell instantly the number of days in any particular month? The number of days in each month is not learned on learning the rhyme, but must be found out on each occasion by a long, indirect process. It is just as though it were necessary to watch a screen, as it is drawn past us, for the printed information; and if by chance the eye failed to catch sight of the desired notice from among the other numerous notices, the screen had to be made to pass in the same way again, not admitting of being drawn backwards.

Let no one therefore deceive himself into thinking that he is loading his mind with information when he instusts to his motor nerves the keeping of knowledge; he is no more doing so than is he who writes in his note-book matters which he thinks he cannot remember. Indeed, in the latter case, the matters, if occasionally reviewed, are soon assimilated by the intellect, and the necessity for memoranda is done away with; but that which is written in the motor system is very slowly— often never—*intellectually* learned."—C. T. DeBrisay, B. A.

Now we see that in a manner, we have two memories. In the difficult work of mastering a language, we need to resort to arts such as parsing in order to make use of the two memories, i. e. to utilize the two powers of the memory. When we parse the spoken or written sentences of correct speakers, we use the *psychical* until the work becomes a child's play to us, then, we parse very much by *motor* memory. Then when we parse at sight, that is, know the parts of speech at a glance, and quote a law of grammar, regarding the forms of the words and regarding the arrangement, we are in a position to employ our knowledge readily in talks of our own. When a thought arises in our minds, a sentence to express it by nature collects in its wake, this sentence we can now parse at a flash, and make any necessary changes, if the laws of grammar applied prove it wanting. By and by this becomes second nature to us, that is, we do it mainly by *motor* memory. But to make correct expression easy, there is another useful practice called

SYNTHESIS.

This practice first employs the *psychical* memory, then the *motor* memory. The mastering of a language is above called difficult, so to speak, but when we diligently make use of Analysis, Parsing, and Synthesis, difficulties will disappear like dew before a burning sun.

SYNTHESIS.

Synthesis is the making of sentences. The term is often applied to the constructing of sentences of given or appointed parts as are below.

The pupil is advised to begin the study and practice of Synthesis soon.

Analysis and Parsing also may be begun early, and the teacher should appreciate the effort rather than the quality of the work.

FUNCTION AGAIN AND FORMS

It has already been told that words are divided into classes according to their functions. Words have general func tions and special functions. For instance, the word books, besides reminding us of an object which we know, tells us also that more than one is referred to. Book and books are different forms of the same word. In a manner, books is the special form of the word, but either is usually taken as the special form, for the form that is used at any time performs the special function, or has the special sense required. The same may be said of tree, trees, child, children, write, wrote, written, etc., and of all different forms of the same word.

Change of form in Nouns and Pronouns is called Declension. Conjugation is the name given to change of form in Verbs, and change of form in Adverbs is called Comparison.

DECLENSION OF NOUNS.

Nouns have two declensions, namely, Number and Gender.

Number signifies that a Noun that stands for one person or thing differs clearly, yet very little, from a word that stands for two or more persons or things. The difference may be a slight sound. If the words be printed or written the difference is represented in the spelling. In the sentence, I gave him one book for two books, there are two words that look alike, book and books. A philologist would call book and books, each a different form of the same word. But a grammarian considers them as two words for he deals with words as they are or ought to be, not as they were ages ago. But, strange to say, some Nouns do not indicate whether they stand for one person or thing or more than one. For instance, see the word salmon, in these sentences, I saw a salmon. I saw twenty salmon. The difference in the meaning is effected by other words. All such words are neither singular nor plural, etymologically, but for certain reasons we may call them Nouns of either Number, singular or plural sense, according to their functions.

The philologist says that the form of the word which denotes one object was made first. The gramarian, therefore, considers the singular word the standard, and the plural word the variation. So we say that the plural is usually formed by suffixing s (or es) to the singular; but we never say that the singular is formed by curtailing s (or es) from the plural.

There are five kinds of Nouns that are put in the plural appearance by suffixing es.

(1.)   Nouns ending in s, sh, soft ch, x or z.

(2.)   Nouns ending in y when this y has a consonant or que, and when this es to be added i is placed in the place of y.

(3.)   Some Nouns ending in o.

(4.)   Some Nouns ending in f.

(5.)   Some Nouns ending in i.

The plural sign for the word ox is en, and that for the word child is ren.

There are some Nouns that take either of two plural signs. The words thus made differ in meaning according to the sign used. The following is an illustration:—

Singular.	Plural.
Brother	Brothers, by birth
	brethren, of the same society.
Cloth	cloths, varieties of cloth
	clothes, garments.
Die	dies, stamps for coining
	dice, cubes for gaming.
Genius	geniuses, men of genius
	genii, fabled spirits.
Index	indexes, table of contents
	indices, algebraic signs.
Pea	peas, single seeds
	pease, the grain as a species.
Penny	pennies, separate coins
	pence, value or amount.
Shot	shots, discharges
	shot, balls or bullets.

Letters, figures and other characters, used as Nouns have apostrophe (') and s as their plural sign. For example, Dot that i. Dot the two i's.

Here are three other words that do not follow the law first given for the expressing of the plural:—

Singular.	**Plural.**
Cherub.	cherubim.
Seraph.	seraphim.
Beau.	beaux.

NOTE.—In any part of speech whose meaning may be influenced by Number, we parse it "Either Number", if the rest of the sentence does not show whether it is singular or plural, as, You are smart. Here, you and are, are each of Either Number.

CLASSES OF NOUNS.

There are two great classes of Nouns, namely, Individual and General.

An Individual Noun is a name used to distinguish one person or thing from others of the same kind by the mere name without using any word to express description. The words James, George, Montreal and Strathlorne are examples.

A General Noun is a name given to objects which distinguishes them from different objects, but not from others of the same kind. For example, observe the words man, city, land.

There is a class of General Nouns distinguished from the rest by the name Collective, and they are known as General Nouns, Collective. One particular law of grammar refers to this class and the term Collective is employed for the sake of convenience in expressing and applying the law.

A Collective Noun is a name which stands for a number of individuals taken as a mass, and sometimes spoken of as a single obejct. The words, herd, jury, parliament and cabinet are examples.

Gender is a property which we may give to a word to show that we mean one of womankind, not of mankind. For instance, authoress, editress, Sultana.

Gender is sometimes, but seldom, a property of a word denoting one of mankind. For instance, bridegroom.

Gender is also a property of words denoting animals of the female sex, and sometimes, but rarely, a word denoting one of the male sex has Gender. For instance, Billy goat, he bear.

There are two Genders, the Masculine and the Feminine. Words of the Feminine Gender are much more plentiful. No No word in its original form has Gender.

Here follow some words of the Feminine and of the Masculine, which may be useful in speaking and writing:—

Masculine.	Feminine.
Abbot	abbess
Actor	actress
Adjutor	adjutrix
Administrator	administratrix
Adventurer	adventuress
Ambassador	ambassadress
Arbiter	arbitress
Auditor	auditress
Augustus	Augusta
Author	authoress
Baron	baroness
Beau	belle
Benefactor	benef ctress
Billy-goat	nanny-goat
Bridegroom	bride
Buck-rabbit	doe-rabbit
Canon	canoness
Caterer	cateress
Chanter	chantress
Charles	Charlotte *or* Caroline
Coadjutor	coadjutrix
Cock-sparrow	hen-sparrow
Colt *or* foal	filly
Conductor	conductress
Count	countess
Czar	czarina
Dauphin	dauphiness
Deacon	deaconess
Director	directress
Don	donna
Drake	duck
Duke	duchess
Editor	editress
Elector	electress
Embasador	embassadress
or	*or*
Ambassador	ambassadress
Emperor	empress
Enchanter	enchantress
Equestrian	equestrienne
Executor	executrix
Francis	Frances
Gentleman	lady *or* gentlewoman
George	Georgiana
Giant	giantess

Masculine.	Feminine.
God	goddess
Governor	governess
Grandfather	grandmother
He-bear	she-bear
Heir	heiress
Henry	Henrietta *or* Harriet
Heritor	heritrix
Hero	heroine
Hunter	huntress
Idolator	idolatress
Infante { A Spanish prince }	infanta
Instructor	instructress
Inventor	inventress
Jesse	Jessie
Jew	Jewess
John	Jane, Joan *or* Joanna
Joseph	Josephine
Julius	{ Julia / Juliet }
Langrave	Landgravine
Landlord	landlady
Louis	{ Louisa / Louise }
Lucius	Lucy
Man	woman
Man-servant	maid-servant
Marquis	marchioness
Mayor	mayoress
Master	mistress
Merman	mermaid
Monitor	monitress
Mr.	Mrs. *or* Miss
Murderer	murderess
Negro	negress
Nephew	niece
Ogre	ogress
Patron	patroness
Preceptor	preceptress
Peer	peeress
Porter	portress
Prince	princess
Prior	prioress
Prophet	prophetess
Prosecutor	prosecutrix
Protector	protectress
Signore { pronounced *seen'yur* }	signora
Signor	

Masculine			Feminine.
Shepherd			shepherdess
Songster			songsteress
Sorcerer			sorceress
Sultan			{ sultana { sultaness
Tempter			temptress
Testator			testatrix
Traitor			traitoress
Tutor			tutoress
Victor			{ victoria { victress
Viscount	{ pronounced { *Vi'kount*	}	viscountess
Votary			votaress
Wizard			witch

The word gentleman shows Gender, because from the word we infer that a man is meant. Gentlewoman has Gender for the same reasons. The word authoress has Gender, because the ending, ess, suggests the female sex.

When we look at a Noun, or Pronoun, and without consulting connected words, if we can glean from its form the sex of the object, the word has Gender, as she, lioness, he-goat.

Yet it is customary to class words which we know to stand for males as Masculine; words standing for females, Feminine; words standing for neither, Neuter Gender; and words such as people, folk, family, child, which may be used to stand for one or more of either, or both sexes, are said to be of the Common Gender.

THE ADJECTIVE.

Adjectives are of four kinds, Descriptive, Limiting, Possessive and Appositive.

Descriptive Adjvectives merely describe. For example, Good roads. Red birds. Little bushes.

Limiting Adjectives do not describe but they set limits to the number of objects for which the Noun stands. For example, Few people. These hens. Those books. Every boy. Each day. All hands.

Possessive Adjectives are words used to express possession. For example, my, thy, her, its, our, their and your; James's, London's, May's, The three *boys'* coats.

An Appositive Adjective is a Noun in form, but is often used as an Adjective for the purpose of description, definition or explanation. For instance, I saw the poet, Byron. There are Appositive Adjective Compounds. For instance, I **saw** Byron, the great poet. If the elements of the Compound, "the great poet," be classified or parsed *Byron* becomes a Noun and *great* its Adjective.

SUB-CLASSIFICATION OF ADJECTIVES.

Limiting and Descriptive Adjectives are sub-classed into Positive, Comparative and Superlative Adjectives. There are three kinds of Limiting Adjectives and three kinds of Descriptive Adjectives, therefore, the names Positive, Comparative and Superlative are necessary that we make use of the laws of language regarding Limiting and Descriptive Adjectives.

The Positive Adjective is used to limit or describe, without suggesting any comparison. For instance, A *strong* box. Few boxes.

The Comparative Adjective is one which not only limits, or describes, but moreover shows comparison with something else. For instance, A stronger box. Fewer boxes.

The Superlative Adjective, besides limiting, or describing, shows an object's comparison with more than one object. For instance, That is the strongest box of the three.

FORMATION OF COMPARATIVE AND SUPERLATIVE ADJECTIVES.

The Positive Adjective is taken as the standard. The most of the Positive Adjectives become Comparative if er be added to them, and Superlative if est be added to them. For instance, strong, stronger, strongest. The learner will do well to remember that the grammarian regards strong, stronger, strongest as different words. The philologist regards them as different forms of the same word.

In the formation of Comparative and Superlative Adjectives out of Positive Adjectives by means of er and est, a final consonant is doubled, final e is dropped, and final y is changed into i. For instance, hot, hotter, hottest; wise, wiser, wisest, not wise, wiseer, wiseest; happy, happier, happiest. But there are a few exceptions: coy, coyer, coyest; sweet, sweeter, sweetest.

The formation of Comparative and Superlative Adjectives by the use of er and est is almost limited to words of one and two syllables. Forms of more than three syllables and even forms of three syllables are formed by prefixing more and most. The object of this formation is to prevent harshness of sound. For instance, more powerful, most powerful is more melodious than powerfuler, powerfulest.

There are two classes of dissyllabic (two syllable) Positive Adjectives that become Comparative and Superlative by the suffixing of er and est.

(1.) Those accented on the second syllable. For instance, divine, diviner, divinest; polite, politer, politest.

(2.) Those ending in y, ble, er and ow. For instance, lovely, lovelier, loveliest; able, abler, ablest; tender, tenderer, tenderest; narrow, narrower, narrowest.

There are a few cases where the formation of the Comparative and Superlative Adjectives is left at the option of the speaker or writer. For instance, handsomer, handsomest are as melodious as more handsome, most handsome.

A number of Positive Adjectives cannot be made Comparative and Superlative by merely adding er and est. The nature of the Comparatives and Superlatives corresponding to these Positives may be gleaned from the following table:—

Positive **Adj.**	Comp. **Adj.**	Super. **Adj.**
Betan *or* Good	better	betest *or* best.
Bad Evil Ill	worse	worst
Little	less	east!
Much Many	more	most
Far	farther	farthest
Hinder	hinder	bindest
In	inner	inmost *or* innermost
Out	outer *or* utter	utmost *or* uttermost
Fore	former	foremost *or* first
Late	later, latter	latest *or* last
Forth	further	furtherest
Neath	neither	nethermost.

The Positive Adjective, old, has two Comparatives and two Superlatives.

Old	older elder	oldest eldest.

Older and oldest are applied to persons and things. Elder and eldest are chiefly used with reference to members of the same family.

Sometimes a person or an object has a certain quality and another person or object has the same quality but in a lesser extent. We also may meet with a person, or an object, that has a certain quality in lesser extent than two or more other persons or objects have. This is sometimes called comparative diminution. For example:—

Pos. Adj.	Com. Adj.	Sup. Adj.
Wise	less wise	least wise
Strong	less strong	least strong
Big	less big	least big
Sweet	less sweet	least sweet
Profound	less profound	least profound.

SUB-CLASSIFICATION OF PRONOUNS.

There are six kinds of Pronouns:—Personal, introducing, question, demonstrative, indefinite and reciprocal.

THE PERSONAL PRONOUNS.

The Personal Pronouns are I, thou, he, she, it, me, we, us, ye, you, thee, they and them.

The word *I* denotes the speaker, and is called a First Personal Pronoun.

Thou denotes the person spoken to, and is called the Second Personal Pronoun.

He and she denote persons spoken of, and are called Third Personal Pronouns.

The word *it* sometimes denotes a child, and more often? an object, or thing, of inferior rank or without life. *It* is a Third Personal Pronoun. He, she and it have *they* for a plural word. You may say of two sticks that *they* are hard.

The learner will do well to master the table below. It will help in the proper manner of employing the Personal Pronouns, in speaking and writing. Before coming to the table it is fair to tell the learner that there are two great classes of Personal Pronouns, namely, the Nominative and the Objective.

Nominative Personal Pronouns are those used as subjects of statements. For instance, *He* is well. *I* see you. *You* are smart.

Objective Personal Pronouns are those which stand for persons, or things, that were objects of action. For instance, John struck *me*. I struck *you*. These also may be objects of Prepositions, as, I went *under* the arch.

DECLENSION OF PERSONAL PRONOUNS.

First Person.

Nom.	Poss. Adj.	Obj.	Nom.	Poss. Adj.	Obj.
I	my *or* mine	me	we	our *or* ours	us

Second Person.

You	your *or* yours	you	you	your *or* yours	you

Third Person.

Mas.	He	his	him ⎫	they	their *or* theirs	them
Fem.	She ·	her *or* hers	her ⎬	they	their *or* theirs	them
No.	It	its	it ⎭			

In the above table, my, mine, thy, thine, your, yours, our, ours, their and theirs are Possessive Adjectives.

COMPOUND PERSONAL PRONOUNS.

The Compound Personal Pronouns are formed by adding self (plural selves) to my, your and him, her and it. For instance:

	Singular	Plural.
First Person	Myself	Ourselves
Second Person	Yourself	Yourselves
	Himself ⎫	
Third Person	Herself ⎬	Themselves
	Itself ⎭	

Their use is *reflexive*, that is, to reflect or bend back upon the person or thing spoken of, in connection with the action expressed by the Verb.

When they are used for emphasis, they are *Adjectives*. For instance, He, *himself*, did it. We, *ourselves*, are to blame.

INTRODUCING PRONOUNS.

An Introducing Pronoun is one often used as the first word of a Post Compound, and which moreover stands for a preceding Noun or Pronoun or Compound. This preceding Noun or Pronoun is called an *antecedent*. The introducing Pronouns are, who, which, what and that.

In the following sentences the functions of Introducing Pronouns may be seen:—I saw the man, *who* made the cart. The horse, *which* you saw, is mine. Tell him, *what* you mean. There is the man *that* struck you.

Who is applied to persons, or the higher intelligences generally. *Which* is applied to animals and objects without life. *That* is used when it would be improper to use who or which, or when the repetition of either becomes offensive. The subjective word *who* has the object form *whom*, and there is a corresponding Adjective form *whose*.

That is used to represent both persons and things in introducing restrictive Adjective Post Compounds. For instance, Uneasy lies the head, *that* wears a crown.

That as a restrictive introducer should not be used when the antecedent is a proper name, or the name of anything well known. For instances, Wellington *who* (not *that*) is buried in St. Pauls, was a great general.

Some of the uses of *ha* will be better understood by the learner, when he (or she) arrives at Analysis. Here suffice to say, that *that* is used in preference to who or which:

(1.) When there are two or more antecedents standing for persons and things.

(2.) When *who* or *which* would be ambiguous from inability to determine whether the force is intended to be restrictive or continuative. For instance, I received ten dollars from my brothers *who* are in London. If we use *that*, the Post Compound *that are in London*, will mean that the speaker has brothers in London and brothers somewhere else. In the sentence, I received, etc., we don't know whether the speaker has brothers outside of London or not. The speaker, perhaps, means only to throw us the news of their being in London, with the news of the money received.

That is used after the Question Pronoun, *who?* And after *some, any, each, every, all, only*, and *Superaltive Adjectives*.

What, as an Introducing Pronoun, stands only for things and is usually used when the antecedent is omitted, particularly when it is indefinite. In other words, *what* introduces a Post Compound descriptive of something not mentioned—or of nothing in particular. For instance, in the sentence, We should always do *what* is right. *What* is not put for anything definite. There are many things right and life would be too short to do everything that is right. So you see *what* has no particular antecedent in the sentence given. But should it have a particular antecedent the latter is left unsaid.

Exercise.

Find the Pronouns in the following sentences, classify them and give the Number and the Gender. (To classify may be enough first).

I saw you before. He is my friend. It flew away. Buy me a hat. Whoever told you made a mistake. He gave the man a book, which was the first that he ever read. Let us go. Who is that person? What is the matter? Whom do you

see? ·'They love each other. None are ready·to come. One'
ought to be able·to read. He will'not speak to either, (more.)'
NOTE.—In a few cases, *What* is used when the antecedent
is expressed. For instance, That book is what I read.

INTRODUCING PRONOUNS.

Certain compound forms have been produced by adding
the words so and ever seither eparately or combined to the
simple Introducing Pronouns who, or whom, or to the Ajective
whose. They are whoso, whosoever, whoever, whatever and
whatsoever. The subjective form whosoever has whomsoever
for its objective form. The Adjective form is whosesoever.
These words are dropping out of use.

OTHER INTRODUCING PRONOUNS.

The word *as* is an Introducing Pronoun, when it introduces
a restrictive clause following the words *such* or *same*. For
instance, You will always find him such *as* he professes to be.
The word *but* is an introducing Pronoun when following a
negative antecedent. For instance, There is no one, *but* will
admit that. In this sentence *but* is subject of will and the Post
Compound *but will admit that* is an Adj. Post Compound.

Exercise.—Name and Classify the Introducing Pronouns.

He lives just the same as you were told. There is no
house but has one vacant chair. John will reward whoever will
help him. The horse which you bought was once mine. You
are the person who is to blame. We told him what he ought
to do. I know whom you mean. The man, who proved to be
a hero, went with him to camp. There are not but will believe
you. This thing is what you want.

QUESTION PRONOUNS.

A Question Pronoun is one used in asking questions.
There are three of them, *who*, *which* and *what*. *Who* has· a
subject and an object form, *who* and *whom*. For instance:
Who is there? *Whom* did you strike? There is, also, an Adjective form *whose*. For instance: *Whose* horse is that?
Which is used in asking questions about qualities,
lower animals, and things. For instance: *Which* horse is the
faster? *Which* stone is the heaviest? *Which* speed do you
prefer?
What is a Question Pronoun used in asking a question,
but not about any particular thing, *what* gives a question a
wide range admitting of many different answers. For instance:
What is man? *What* do you need?

Find the Question Pronouns in the following sentences: Who are you? What are you? Whom do you see? Which do you prefer? What do you do? Who is your father?

The Indefinite Pronouns are *one, none, either, neither*.

The Reciprocal Pronouns are *each, other, one, another*.

CLASSIFICATION OF VERBS

There are two classes of Verbs, Affecting and Unaffecting.

Affecting Verbs are those which express action that affects something other than the Subject. For instance: He hit the bear.

This affecting may be a creation, as, He wrote a letter.
Again, the affecting may be a figure of Language, that is an affecting merely in fancy; as I heard music. I love you. I see nothing.
An Unaffecting Verb expresses state, existence, or condition which affects no object in fact or fancy, as, I sleep. John runs.
Of course the same word may be an Affecting Verb in one statement and an Unaffecting Verb in another, as, James drives, for he hates walking. James drives passengers.
In all sentences, the part that denotes what we speak, or write, about, is called the Subject.
The predicate is what is said by the material Subject, or about the Subject, as, I see you. John fell.
The Predicate is not always in the same relation to the Subject.
Voice is the name given to the relationship of the Predicate to the subject. In other words, Voice is the relationship of a Verb to the Noun or Pronoun with which it must agree in Number and Person. Such Verbs are called Finite Verbs, when so used, but are not Finite Verbs in the dictionary, or taken alone.
There are two kinds of Voice, Active and Passive. The words Active Voice mean, Active in Voice.
When the person, or thing, denoted by the Subject performs the action the Verb is Active, as, I found him.
When the Subject is affected by the Active Adverb used with a verb, the two words make the Passive, as, I was driven. He is praised.
By a little study, it may be seen that in the above sentences, *driven* and *praised* are Active Adverbs. No one would presume to call me a driven man. But in what state was I existing? I was *driven*. Driven explains, therefore, it is an

Adverb. I was driven, may be parsed thus, I, Pron. First Personal Sing. Number, Common Gender, Nominative, **Subject** of am.

Am Verb **Unaffecting**⎫ No Voice, Declarative Mood
Strong Conjugation. ⎬ Past Tense, First Pers. Sing.
Parts be, was, been. ⎭ like the Subject.
NOTE.—Unaffecting Verbs have no voice. Driven, Adverb, Active of manner modifying *am* and forming with was the Passive form.

MOOD.

Mood is a slight shade of change of meaning in a Verb depending upon the nature of the rest of the sentence. There are six Moods.
Declarative, as, *I* see you.
Question, as, *Is* he here?
Commanding, as *Go* in.
Conditional, as, Unless you WORK, starve.
Wish, as, May God bless you!
Exclamatory, Hear me for my cause!
The Declarative Mood tells.
The Question Mood asks.
The Commanding Mood orders, requests, or commands.
The Conditional Mood is used in Post Compounds, where there is a condition, doubt, or contingency expressed.
The Plural form of the Declarative Verb is used in the Conditional Mood, as, unless he go, I shall not be happy. If he were here, he would work. Sometimes the root of a Verb is used. If he are elected, is not correct, say if he be elected.
The Wish Mood is used in wishes, as, May you be happy. Long *live* the King.
The Exclamatory Mood, is employed to show wonder, joy, etc., in a simple, but emphatic way, as Woe to them! O, hear him now!
In the sentence, May God bless him! May is in the commanding (or requesting Mood); but bless discloses and asserts the wish, and is of the wish Mood.
May God bless him, is like, Thou God, please do bless him, or, God bless him. May is Second Pers. Singular. Bless is an Infinitive, Active Voice. Wish Mood, Present Tense. Object of may. Study, I permit things.
Tell the Mood of each Verb in the following sentences:—
Come here, Flora. Give me a drink. If he stay, I'll go. Where are you? John struck the table. James came home. If he were home, he might help you. Unless you reply to my letters, I shall not write. Though he strike you, love him still.

A REMARK ON THE CONDITIONAL MOOD.

In form the Conditional Mood is like the Plural of the Declarative Mood. For instance: Two men were seen. If one man *were* seen, I would go.

· Again suppose a man was daily, coming .to see. you, it would be not correct to say though he come. Though he comes, is correct. When the condition etc. is being fulfilled continuatively, or at intervals, the Verb follows the rules of *number like the Declarative Mood.*

TENSE.

Tense is a property of Verbs which indicates whether a state, or action, existed, or took place, in the past, or exists, or takes place, at the present time.

Tense is also a property of statements to which Shall, or Will, or their past equals Should or Would are prefixed. For instance: I shall work. You will write. You would write.

Tense is moreover, a property of Post Compounds and of sentences. For instance:—

I am driving.—Present Progressive Tense.
I have been.— Perfect.
I drive.— Grand Present.

Except Shall and Will, no Verb can have but two tenses, the Present and the Past. For instance: Write, wrote; see, saw; laugh, laughed; run, ran; mail, mailed.

Shall's Past is Should and the Past of Will is Should. Again Shall and Will are some times of the Present Tense and some times refer to time to come. They are then of the Future Tense.

There are three grand divisions of time, the Past, Present, Future. Grammar gives a construction for each division, the third or Future Tense being effected by introducing another word that is Shall or Will. These are called the Grand Tenses. There are moreover the Intermediate Tenses.

When the subject of *Shall* is a First Personal Pronoun, Shall is in the Future Tense. When the subject of Shall is Second or Third Personal, it is in the Present Tense. Will is Present in the First Person, and Future, in the Second and Third.

When Will is in the Present Tense it means, resolved or determined. When Shall is in the Present Tense it means, obliged or bound or compelled by a superior authority or impelled by circumstances.

As Present Tenses, Shall and Will, have Should and Would for their Past Tenses. From the nature of the case it is manifest that as Future Tenses, they usually need no corresponding Past Tenses, but in telling the statements of former times in Indirect Transposition style the Future Tenses Shall and Will may be transposed into Should and Would. For instance, I say, I shall go. He said, he should go. I tell you, I will go. He told him (or her) he would go. Therefore these Pasts do not follow the laws of Person of their Futures.

As already hinted, the future has no past. But we view past and future from a present standpoint. And if we refer to the future now, from a present standpoint, we may regard that reference as a past affair at any moment from a present standpoint. For instance:—

Future Indefinite Tense.

I shall drive.	We shall drive.
You will drive.	You will drive.
He will drive.	They will drive.

Past.

I should drive.	We should drive.
You would drive.	You would drive.
He would drive.	They would drive.

In such cases, *would* takes the place of will in the second and third persons.

In asking questions, if you expect the answer I shall go, say, Shall you go? If you expect I will go (I am determined to go) say. Will you go?

Shall and Will are Affecting Verbs. They take the Infinitiev for Object. They say something about the Infinitive. In all cases, the Object is a kind of secondary subject which has sometimes more prominence than anything else. Now in the sentence, I shall go, nothing is done to go but something is said about it as in the sentence, I see the sun, something is said of the sun.

It matters not whether Shall and Will are used as Present, Past or Future Tenses, they are always Affecting.

STRONG AND WEAK VERBS.

Regular and Irregular Verbs.

The *past tenses* of some Verbs were formed and settled by the common people, etc., in England long before a rule was made for their formation. Therefore these do not follow any particular rule for the formation of the past and derived Adverb or Infinitive. Those that form the past by a change of root vowel and whose derived Adv. or Infin. usually ends in en, are called Strong Verbs. Those that form the past, etc., as seen later on, table I ,are called Weak. Irregular Weak Verbs follow no rule for the formation of the past tense and derived Adverb or Infinitive.

The great majority of Verbs form the past, etc., by adding d or ed to the present. These also are called Weak Verbs. The words weak and strong have no meaning 'hus used, save that they serve as distinctions.

Strong Verbs are those whose past is formed by a change of root vowel. For instance, write, wrote. The derived Adverb or Infinitive usually ends in en, but not always. For instance, written, won.

NOTE.—In the sentence, I am driven, driven is an Adverb of state or Manner. In the sentence, I have driven, driven is an Infinitive, Object of have.

PERSON.

Person is a property of Verbs which has grown out of usage, a property which varies in the Singular according to the nature of the Personal Pronoun, or its Relative, which may be the Subject. For instance, I am. You are. He is.

But Verbs of the Plural Number are supposed to have Person though the property is not manifest. For instance, the Verb *are* is First, Second and Third Personal, successively, in the following sentences:—We are. You are. They are.

NUMBER.

Number is a property of Verbs, a real property not always manifest, corresponding to the Number of the Subject. For instance, the man *talks*. The men *talk*. I drive. We drive. He drives. If he *drive*, I shall be happy.

The Singular Verb often ends in s.

TABLE I.

Present.	Past.	Corresponding Adv. *or* Infin. *or* Adj.
Bend	bent	bent
Bereave	bereft	bereft
Beseech	besought	besought
Bet	bet	bet
Bleed	bled	bled
Blend	blent	blent
Breed	bred	bred
Bring	brought	brought

Present.	Past.	Corresponding Adv. *or* Infin. *or* Adj.
Build	built	built
Burst	burst	burst
Burn	burnt	burnt
Buy	bought	bought
Cast	cast	cast
Catch	caught	caught
Clothe	clad	clad
Cleave (trans)	cleft	cleft
Cost	cost	cost
Creep	crept	crept
Cut	cut	cut
Deal	dealt	dealt
Dream	dreamt	dreamt
Dwell	dwelt	dwelt
Feed	fed	fed
Feel	felt	felt
Flee	fled	fled
Gild	gilt	gilt
Gird	girt	girt
Have	had	had
Hear	heard	heard
Hit	hit	hit
Hurt	hurt	hurt
Keep	kept	kept
Kneel	knelt	knelt
Knit	knit	knit
Lay	laid	laid
Lead	lead	lead
Leap	leapt	leapt
Learn	learnt	learnt
Leave	left	left
Lend	lent	lent
Let	let	let
Light	lit	lit
Lose	lost	lost
Make	made	made
Mean	meant	meant
Meet	met	met
Pay	paid	paid
Put	put	put
Pen	pent	pent
Read	read ·	read
Rend	rent	rent
Rid	rid	rid
Say	said	said
Seek	sought	sought

Present	Past	Corresponding Adv. or Infin. or Adj.
Sell	sold	sold
Send	sent	sent
Set	set	set
Shed	shed	shed
Shoe	shod	shod
Shred	shred	shred
Shut	shut	shut
Sleep	slept	slept
Slit	slit	slit
Speed	sped	sped
Spell	spelt	spelt
Spend	spent	speht
Spill	spilt·	spilt
Spit	spit	spit
Split	split	split
Spread	spread	spread
Stay	stay	stay
Sweep	swept	swept
Sweat	sweat	sweat
Teach	taught	taught
Tell	told	told
Think	thought	thought
Thrust	thrust	thrust
Wed	wed	wed
Weep	wept	wept
Wet	wet	wet
Whet	whet	whet
Work	wrought	wrought

STRONG VERBS.

TABLE II.

Present.	Past.	Corresponding Adv. or Infin. or Adj.
Abide	abode	abode
Arise	arose	arisen
Awake	awoke	awaken
Bear (give birth)	bore,	born
Bear (to carry)	bore, bare	borne
Beat	beat	beaten
Begin	began	begun
Behold	beheld	beholden or beheld
Bid	bade, bid	bidden or bid
Bind	bound	bound

Present.	Past.	Corresponding Adv. *or* Infin. *or* Adj.
Bite	bit	bitten *or* bit
Blow	blew	blown
Break	broke	broken
Chide	chid	chidden *or* chid
Choose	chose	chosen
Cleave (split)	cloven	cloven
Cling	clung	clung
Come	came	come
Crow	crew	crown
Dig	dug	dug
Do	did	done
Draw	drew	drawn
Drink	drank	drunk
Drive	drove	driven
Eat	ate	eaten
Fall	fell	fallen
Fight	fought	fought
Find	found	found
Fling	flung	flung
Fly	flew	flown
Forbear	forbore	forborne
Forbid	forbade	forbidden
Forget	forgot	forgotten
Forsake	forsook	forsaken
Freeze	froze	frozen
Get	got, gotten	got
Give	gave	given
Go	went	gone
Grave	graved	graven
Grind	ground	ground
Grow	grew	grown
Hang	hung	hung
Heave	heaved	heaved
Hew	(hewed)	hewn
Hide	hid, hidden	hid
Hold	held, holden	held
Know	knew	known
Lade	(laded)	laden *or* loaden
Lie	lay	lain
Ride	rode	ridden
Ring	rang	rung
Rise	rose	risen
Rive	(rived)	riven
Run	ran	run
See	saw	seen
Seethe	sod	sodden

Present	Past.	Corresponding Adv. or Infin. or Adj.
Shake	shook	shaken
Shave	(shaved)	shaven
Shear	shore	shorn
Shine	shone	shone
Shrink	shrank	shrunk
Sing	sang	sung
Sink	sank	sunk
Sit	sat	sat
Slay	slew	slain
Slide	slid	slidden or slid
Sling	slung	slung
Slink	slunk	slunk
Smite	smote	smitten
Sow	(sowed)	sown
Speak	spoke	spoken
Spin	spun	spun
Spring	sprang	sprung
Stand	stood	stood
Steal	stole	stolen
Stick	stuck	stuck
Sting	stung	stung
Stink	stank	stunk
Stride	strode	stridden
Strike	struck	struck, stricken
String	strung	strung
Strive	strove	striven
Swear	swore	sworn
Swell	(swelled)	swollen
Swim	swam	swum
Swing	swung	swung
Take	took	taken
Tear	tore	torn
Thrive	throve	thriven
Throw	threw	thrown
Tread	trod	trodden
Wake	woke	(waked)
Wear	wore	worn
Weave	wove	woven
Win	won	won
Wind	wound	wound
Wring	wrung	wrung
Write	wrote	written

APPROVED PREDICATES.

HAVE

DECLARATIVE MOOD.

Present Tense.

Singular.	*Plural.*
I have	We have.
You have	Ye *or* you have.
He *or* John has.	Men *or* they have.

Past Tense.

Singular.	*Plural.*
I had.	We had.
You had.	Ye *or* you had.
He *or* John has.	Men *or* they have.

CONDITIONAL MOOD.

Present Tense.

Singular.	*Plural.*
(If) I have.	(If) We have.
(If) You have.	(If) Ye *or* you have.
(If) He have.	(If) Men *or* they have.

SHALL.

Present Tense.

Singular.	*Plural.*
I shall.	We shall.
You shall.	You shall.
He *or* James shall.	They shall.

Past Tense.

Singular.	*Plural.*
I should	We should.
You should.	You should.
He *or* James should.	Men *or* they should.

WILL.

Present Tense.

Singular.	*Plural.*
I will.	He will.
You will.	You will.
He *or* Ann will.	Men *or* they will.

Past Tense.

Singular.   *Plural.*

I would.	We would.
You would.	You would.
He *or* George would.	Men *or* they would.

Present Tense.

Singular.   *Plural.*

I do.	We do.
You do.	You do.
He *or* James does.	They *or* men do.

Past Tense.

Singular.   *Plural.*

I did.	We did.
You did.	You did.
He *or* James did.	Men *or* they did.

BE
DECLARATIVE MOOD.
Present Tense.

Singular.   *Plural.*

I am.	We are.
You are.	You are.
He is.	They *or* men are.

Present Perfect Tense

Singular.   *Plural.*

I have been.	We have been.
You have been.	You have been.
John *or* he has been.	Men *or* they have been.

Past Tense.

Singular.   *Plural.*

I was.	We were.
You were.	You were.
He was.	They *or* men were.

Past Perfect Tense.

Singular.   *Plural.*

I had been.	We had been.
You had been.	You had been.
He *or* John had been.	Men *or* they had been.

Future Tense.

Singular.   *Plural.*

I shall be.   We shall be.
You will be.   You will be.
John *or* he will be.   Men *or* they will be.

Future Perfect Tense.

Singular.   *Plural.*

I shall have been.   We shall have been.
You will have been.   You will have been.
Ann *or* he will have been.   Men *or* they will have been.

CONDITIONAL MOOD.

Present Tense.

Singular.   *Plural.*

(If) I be.   (If) We be.
(If) You be.   (If) You be.
(If) John *or* he be.   (If) Men *or* they be.

Comp. Form.

(If) I should be.   (If) We should be.
(If) You should be.   (If) You should be.
(If) He *or* Ann should be.   (If) They should be.

Present Perfect Tense.

(If) I have been.   (If) We have been.
(If) You have been.   (If) You have been.
(If) Ann *or* he have been.   (If) Men *or* they have been.

Comp. Form.

(If) I should have been.   (If) We should have been.
(If) You should have been.   (If) You should have been.
(If) Ann *or* thye should have been (If) They should have been.

COMMANDING MOOD.

2.   Be (thou aware.)   2nd.   Be (you aware.)

INFINITIVES.

Present Tense—To be.   Present Perfect—To have been.

PARTICIPLES.

Present—Being   Perfect—Having been.   Past—been.

GERUNDS.

Simple—Being.   Compound—Having been.

A collection of constructions where the word work figures prominently as Verb, Adverb and Infinitive. These constructions illustrate the formation of the Grand Tenses, and of the Intermediate Tenses. Any other Verb, such as play, pray, drive, walk, skate may be put in the place of *work*.

DECLARATIVE MOOD.

Principal Parts—Drive, Drove, Derived Adverb or Infinitive Driven.

Present Indefinite Tense.

Singular.	*Plural.*
I work.	We work.
You work.	You work.
John *or* he works.	They work.

Present Progressive Tense.

I am working.	We are working.
You are working.	You are working.
He *or* James is working.	They are working.

Present Perfect.

I have worked.	We have worked.
You have worked.	You have worked.
He has worked.	They have worked.

Present Perfect Progressive.

I have been working.	We have been working.
You have been working.	You have been working.
He has been working.	They have been working.

PAST SYSTEM.

Past Indefinite Tense.

I worked.	We worked.
You worked.	You worked.
He worked.	They worked.

Past Progressive.

Singular.

I was working.
You were working.
He was working.

Plural.

We were working.
You were working.
They were working.

Past Perfect.

I had worked.
You had worked.
He had worked.

We had worked.
You had worked.
They had worked.

Past Perfect Progressive.

I had been working.
You had been working.
He had been working.

We had been working.
You had been working.
They had been working.

FUTURE SYSTEM.

Future Indefinite.

I shall work.
You will work.
He will work.

We shall work.
You will work.
They will work.

Future Progressive.

I shall be working.
You will be working.
He will be working.

We shall be working.
You will be working.
They will be working.

Future Perfect.

I shall have driven.
You will have driven.
He will have driven.

We shall have driven.
You will have driven.
They will have driven.

I shall have been working.
You will have been working.
He will have been working.

We shall have been working.
You will have been working.
They will have been working.

CONDITIONAL MOOD.

Present Indefinite Tense.

Singular.

(If) I work.
(If) You work.
(If) He work.

Plural.

(If) We work.
(If) You work.
(If) They work.

Compound Form.

Singular.   *Plural.*

(If) I should work.   (If) We should work.
(If) You should work.   (If) You should work.
(If) He should work.   (If) They should work.

Present Progressive.

(If) I be working.   (If) We be working.
(If) You be working.   (If) You be working.
(If) He be working.   (If) They be working.

Compound Form.

(If) I should be working.   (If) We should be working.
(If) You should be working.   (If) You should be working.
(If) He should be working   (If) They should be working.

Past Perfect.

(If) I have worked.   (If) We have worked.
(If) You have worked.   (If) You have worked.
(If) He have worked.   (If) They have worked.

Compound Form.

(If) I should have worked.   (If) We should have worked.
(If) You should have worked.   (If) You should have worked.
(If) He should have worked.   (If) They should have worked

Present Perfect Progressive.

(If) I have been working.   (If) We have been working.
(If) You have been working.   (If) You have been working.
(If) He have been working.   (If) They have been working.

Compound Form.

(If) I should have been work-   (If) We should have been
    ing.   working.
(If) You should have been   (If) You should have been
    working.   working.
(If) He should have been   (If) They should have been
    working.   working.

COMMANDING MOOD.

2. Work (you.)   2. Work (you.)

INFINITIVES.

Present Indefinite Tense—To work.
Present Progressive—To be working.
Present Perfect—To have working.
Present Perfect Progressive—To have been working.

PARTICIPLES.

Present—Worknig.
Perfect—Having Worked.
Perfect Progressive—Having been working.

GERUNDS.

Simple—Working.   Compound—Having worked.
    Passive Voice.   Dec. Mood.

PRESENT SYSTEM.

Present Indefinite Tense.

Singular.	*Plural.*
I am worked.	We are worked.
You are worked.	You are worked.
He is worked.	They are worked.

Present Progressive Tense.

I am being worked.	We are being worked.
You are being worked.	You are being worked.
He is being worked.	They are being worked.

Present Perfect.

I have been worked.	We have been worked.
You have been worked.	You have been worked.
He has been worked.	They have been worked.

PAST SYSTEM.

Past Indefinite Tense.

Singular.	*Plural.*
I was worked.	We were worked.
You were worked.	You were worked.
He was worked.	They were worked.

Past Progressive.

Singular. *Plural.*

I was being worked. We were being worked.
You were being worked. You were being worked.
He was being worked. They were being worked.

Past Perfect.

I had been worked. We had been worked.
You had been worked. You had been worked.
He had been worked. They had been worked.

FUTURE SYSTEM.

Future Indefinite Tense.

Singular. *Plural.*

I shall be worked. We shall be worked.
You will be worked. You will be worked.
He will be worked. They will be worked.

Future Perfect.

I shall have been worked. We shall have been worked.
You will have been worked. You will have been worked.
He will have been worked. They will have been worked.

CONDITIONAL MOOD.

Present Indefinite Tense.

Singular. *Plural.*

(If) I be worked. (If) We be worked.
(If) Thou be worked. (If) You be worked.
(If) He be worked. (If) They be worked.

Compound Form.

(If) I should be worked. (If) We should be worked.
(If) You should be worked. (If) You should be worked.
(If) He should be worked (If) They should be worked.

Present Perfect.

(If) I have been worked. (If) We have been worked.
(If) You have been worked) (If) You have been worked.
(If) He have been worked. (If) They have been worked.

Compound Form.

Singular.	*Plural.*
(If) I should have been worked	(If) We should have been worked.
(If) You should have been worked.	(If) You should have been worked.
(If) He should have been worked.	(If) They should have been worked.

PAST SYSTEM.

Past Indefinite Tense.

Singular.	*Plural.*
(If) I were worked.	(If) We were worked.
(If) You were worked.	(If) You were worked.
(If) He were worked.	(If) They were worked.

Past Progressive.

(If) I were being worked.	(If) We were being worked.
(If) You were being worked.	(If) You were being worked.
(If) He were being worked.	(If) They were being worked.

COMMANDING MOOD.

2.   Be (you) worked.   2.   Be (you) worked.

INFINITIVES.

Present Indefinite Tense—To be worked.
Present Perfect—To have been worked.

PATRICIPLES.

Past Indefinite Tense—Worked.
Past Progressive—Being worked.
Perfect—Having worked.

GERUNDS.

Incomplete—Being worked.   Complete—Having been worked.

ADVERB.

An Adverb is a word whose usual function is to tell how, why, when or where an action was performed. For instance, I walk *fast.* I rode *slowly.* He came *soon.*

Adverbs are also used in description of state. For instance, He is *well*. He is *good*. I am driving. He sleeps soundly.

Adverbs moreover modify Adjectives, and sometimes, but seldom, other Adverbs.

Sometimes Adverbs have a connective sense. Therefore, there are two general classes of Adverbs, Simple and Conjunctive.

These are classified into Adverbs of Time, Place, Manner, Cause and Effect, Degree, Emphasis, Affirmation or Negation, Potentiality, Repetition and Order.

Adverbs of Manner—As, how, however, ill, otherwise, so, thus, well, wisely.

Adverbs of Degree—Almost, altogether, half little, less, least, much, more, most, quite, scarcely, very.

Adverbs of Time—Afterwards, again, ago, always, before, daily, ever, hereafter, late, never, now, presently, seldom, since, sometimes, soon, to-day, when.

Adverbs of Place—Above, back, below, down, elsewhere, far hence, here, hither, thence, there, thither, up, where, whence.

Adverbs of Cause and Effect—Accordingly, hence, thence, therefore, wherefore, whence, why.

Adverbs of Emphasis—Nevertheless, notwithstanding, still, yet.

Adverbs of Affirmation or Negation—Aye, certainly, indeed, nay, no, surely, yea, yes.

Adverbs of Potentiality—Perhaps, possibly, probably.

Adverbs of Repetition and Order—Once, twice, first, second.

Some of the words in the foregoing classes are sub-classified into Positive, Comparative and Superlative Adverbs. For instance, early, earlier, earliest; little, less, least; much, more, most; well, better, best.

The original word is regarded as the Positive. The Comparative and Superlative are the variations. Positive Adverbs may be made Comparative and Superlative by prefixing *More* and *Most*, or *Less* and *Least*. .Positive Adverbs are sometimes made Comparative and Superlative by suffixing *er* and *est.*

Here are a few that follow no rule—they are *irregular.*

Positive.	Comparative.	Superlative.
Well	better	best
Badly,	worse	swort
Much	more	most
Little	less	least
Far	farther	farthest
Forth	further	furthest
Near, nigh	nearer	nearest
Late	later	last

Incorrect.	Correct.
How are you? I am good.	How are your? I am well
Pull stronger.	Pull stronglier.
He writes rapid.	He writes rapidly.
He acted wise.	He acted wisely.

THE PREPOSITION.

The Preposition is a word used to express realtionship, usually that of place between a state or an action and some object. For instance, I am *in* the house. I walked *on* the floor.

Exercises.—Point out the Prepositions in the following sentences:—I am under the tree. I am below the falls. I walked between the two men. I am going to school. This is for use. We looked through the window. The boat came alongside the quay. In spite of you I will return. That is beside the mark. The ship has sailed round the world. You may go instead of me. It is not sufficient for us. They rode inside the coach. He did it out of sheer kindness. We could not come owing to the weather. He ran away from us. He went into the house. He is below the fall. He is at the spring. He fell across the stick. Come under the tree. He is against you in politics. He comes from school. He thinks such doings beneath him. Come over the lake. He walked towards the house. He is within the house.

NOTE.—The Preposition can show relationship between states (or actions) and things only. A relationship between objects exists but this cannot be expressed without verbs. Now the Preposition shows the relation between the being, existing or state of the one object to the other. In some cases the verb may not be used but it is always meant.

A quality, or limit, may bear a relationship to an object but this requires a verb for its expression.

A like remark is applicable to Adverbs.

So Prepositions show relationship between states (or actions) and objects. A man of power is feared. Here *of* is equal to that has power. But *of* may be parsed as showing the relation between objects.

CONJUNCTIONS.

A Conjunction is a word that stands for an imaginary, or supposed, tie of union or disunion, between objects or actions or statement. For instance, John *and* James came. John came *but* James did not come.

Some Conjunctions suggest union only. For instance, John or May will come. Neither Flora nor Annie left. Florence will write or play. Catie Ann can sing, but Dan cannot.

Now the sentence John and James came, is to be taken to mean, John came and James came. Therefore a Conjunction is said to connect sentences.

There are two great classes of Conjunctions, Coordinating and Subordinating.

Coordinating Conjunctions connect sentences of equal order. For instance, John and James are here.

Subordinating Conjunctions join a *subordinate* or *dependent* sentence to that on which it depends. For instance, I shall go, *if* you will stay. Though I came first, he was laughing. After I came, he came.

Exercises.—Find the Conjunctions in the following sentences:—I arrived at the house *before tea was served. I will go unless* you stay. I *heard that you were* going. He waited patiently about till Mary did appear. He took a gun lest the bear would kill him. He is better than I thought him to be. I took them all except the last. You and I were to Port Hood.

Find the Subordinating and the Co-ordinating Conjunctions in the following sentences:—I shall go because I am wanted. You and I were young. I told you that he was coming. Neither he nor his father can write. He went willingly 'for he was well paid. Take care lest you fall in the ditch. The road is bad hence you better remain to-night. If you mean what you say you are honest. He is better than you expected. Since you are ready you better go.

CLASSIFICATION OF COMPOUNDS.

Compounds are of five classes:—Noun, Adjective, Adverb, Conjunction and Preposition Compounds. For instance, He wants to do it, Noun. He went there to do it, Adverb. That is the way to do it, Adjective. I will go *provided that* I get the command. Work hard *so that* you'll escape debt. Here are some Preposition Compounds often met with:—*out of, from out, in respect to, in regard to, according to.* Any Compound that performs the function of a Preposition like those given is a Preposition Compound.

CLASSIFICATION OF POST COMPOUNDS.

Post Compounds are of three kinds Adjective, Noun and Adverb Compounds. For instance, I saw the man that performed the work. He said *that he was glad* to *see you.* He ran *as one runs for his life.*

The Noun Post Compound performs the function of a Noun, the Adverb Post Compound that of an Adverb and the Adjective Post Compound, that of an Adjective.

POST COMPOUNDS FURTHER ILLUSTRATED.

Adjective P. C.—The way, *that you may know it* is to visit him.

Adverb P. C.—I tell you this, *that you may know it.*
Noun P. C.—He tells me *that you may know it.*
Adjective P. C.—This is the time when roses bloom.
Adverb P. C.—*When you go home* I'll tell you about it.
Noun P. C.—I know *when the news first came.*

Exercises.

Find the Noun, Adjective and Adverb Post Compounds. All these lean or depend on other statements.

I know the persons who did it. I knew that he was not there. Where you go, I will go. When I was young, I thought of nothing else but pleasure. I met the gentleman on the street, who told me the whole circumstance. I refuse to say who is my informer. It is not true that he said so. He came in before the moon rose. Unless you hurry, you will miss the boat. Can you tell me the reason why he left. The house is comfortable in every respect except that it wants painting. The circumstance that he was present must not be disregarded. I went there because I desired to. The man who labours is liable to succeed. She is one of the best that I ever saw. She plays the melodeon and the autoharp when she is requested. The Inverness Courier in question is the only one that I have ever seen. I heard that she was in Mull. Tena went to Boston where she intends to spend the winter. That truth is good is not doubted. I remember that it was something about a paper. Strike when the iron is hot. A kind of dread had hitherto kept me b   ; but I was restless now till I had accomplished my work.ack

RULES OF ETYMOLOGY.

Rule 1—When a Pronoun is employed as the subject of a statement, it must be used in its Nominative form. For instance, *Him* is a good boy is incorrect. Say *He* is a good boy.

This rule applies to Personal and Relative Pronouns.

Rule 2.—When a word that is a Noun or Pronoun in form is used after a verb and in function suggestive or descriptive of state it is an Adverb Compound or an Adverb. For instance, You are *the man*. He is *King*. They are *cowards*. You are *he*.

(3)   When a word that is a Noun in form is used with a Noun for the purpose of description or definition it is an Adjective. For instance, The great Emperor, *Bonaparte*, went to Paris.

(4)   When such a word has an Adjective describing, or limiting, it, it is in itself regarded as a Noun, but with its Adjective it is an Adjective Compound. For instance, I˙ saw Waterloo, that field of glory.

(5)   If there is a word denoting a person or thing addressed it is descriptive as well as the word *white*, and is an Adjective. For instance, I tell you, John, you are smart.

(6)   In some cases, a Verb to which ing is suffixed continues to be a Verb still and nothing else. For instance, Clouds *having* obscured the sun, the rest of the journey was more pleasant is the same in meaning as because clouds had obscured, etc., etc.

(7)   A Verb agrees with its subject in number. For instance, John is well. James works.

(8)   Collective Nouns require singular or plural Verbs according as they convey the idea of unity or plurality; as, The Council meets on Monday. The people have lost confidence in the schemes.

(9)   When the subject of a Verb is made of parts joined by *and* the Verb is usually Plural.
Exceptions:

THE VERB IS SINGULAR.

(1)   When *and* simply connect different names of the same person or thing. For instance, That excellent and gifted poet is now forgotten.

(2)   When Nouns, etc. are joined which nearly agree in meaning or denote objects closely connected in fact or in the thought of the speaker. For instance, The peace and good order of the country was not promoted by the feudal system.

(3)   When the words are individualized by the word each or every. For instance, Each officer and each soldier is well

cared for. Every thing to please and every thing to benefit was there in abundance.

(10) When the subject consists of two or more parts joined by *or* the Verb is Singular

(11) A subject composed of more than two parts, and or, or need only be used between the last word and the one next to it. John, Hugh, and Allan went. James, Edward or Hugh is sure to come.

(12) When some parts of a subject joined by or or nor are Singular and others Plural *the Verb agrees with its nearest Subject.*

Some Pronouns have a particular form to indicate the sex of the person or animal for which they stand. For instance, John is liked, because *he* is honest. Possessive Adjectives derived from Pronouns have particular forms to indicate the sex of the owner.

(15) The Demonstrative Adjectives *this* and *that* agree in Number with the Nouns which they limit. For instance, This man. These men.

(16) A word that limits another by expressing ownership is an Adjective and requires apostrophe after it or apostrophe and *s*. For instance, The boy's book is here. The boys' books are here. The curl called apostrophe was invented by printers, and is not old. Strictly the Possessive is formed by *s*.

(17) On a series of Possessive Adjectives, if separate ownership is meant, use or write, each Adjective with the possive sign, if joint ownership, use the sign with the last only.

(18) A Noun followed by an Appositive Adjective or Adj. Compound is not changed into an Adjective to indicate ownership, but the possessive sign is suffixed to the Apositive Adjective, or Apositive Adj. Compound. For instance, Byron, the poet's, writings are admired.

A remark. In such a sentence as, That book of his, his is in function a Noun, and object of the Preposition *of* because his and such words in such cases suggests to the mind the *things* that are his much more than the idea of possession.

(19) A noun denoting an object effected by an Affecting Verb is said to be the object of *that* Verb, and a Noun related to an action, etc by a Perposition is object of the Preposition.

(20) A Pronoun standing for a Noun *that* would be the object of a Verb, or of a Preposition, is in the Objective Case, and takes the Objective form. For instance, He gave the book to *I* is incorrect. Say, he gave the book to *me*.

(21) Allow, bring, deny, do, forgive, get, give, lend, offer, pay promise, refuse, send, tell, take a second object to denote

the person or thing effected by their action. For instance, He told *them*, a sad story.

The first object is called the Indirect obj. The last is called the Direct.

(22) The Verbs ask and teach are usually followed by two objects and are both considered Direct.

(23) If a Verb be *used* Affectingly it is an Affecting Verb. For instance, Seneca lived a virtuous life. In the sentence, John sang himself hoarse. Sang is an Affecting Verb, Hoarse is an Adv. of Deg.

(24) If a Verb is Affecting in function, it may be regarded as Affecting. For instance, Seneca lived a virtuous life, or Unaffecting the supposed object etc. regarded as an Adv. Compound.

(25) What ever be the form of a word, or of the elements of a Compound or Post Compound, if used adverbially, it is an Adverb, Adverb Compound, or Adverb Post Compound.

(26) The Conjunction *than* takes after it the Objective form of the Pronoun *who*.

(27) Some Interjections are followed by the Objective form of the First and the Nominative form of the Second Personal Pronoun. For instance, Ah me! Ho! They that fight .

(28) Infinitives perform double functions, that of Nouns and Verbs, but sometimes they are Adverbs and sometimes Adjectives. For instance, I am able *to finish* what I have begun. His anxiety *to avoid* one class of danger led him into another. In the first sentence, to finish is an Adverb modifying able. In the second sentence, to avoid is an Adjective limiting anxiety.

(29) The Conditional Conjunctions, if, unless, etc., and the Concessive Conjunctions although, though, etc., are followed by the Conditional Mood in clauses denoting future uncertainty. For instance, If he *be* here, I shall see him. If he *were* tried, he would be acquitted. Though he see me, he would not attack me.

(30) Present and Future Tenses in a principal clause require *may, shall* and *will* in the subordinate clause. Past Tenses require *might, should* and *would*. For instance, I come that I *might* attend to this matter, is incorrect, say, I come that I *may* attend to this matter.

RULES OF SYNTAX.

Before giving Rules of Syntax the Fundamental Law of Syntax may be given. First comes the Subject with its En-

largements. Then follow the Verb, the Object and its Enlargements. Finally comes the Extension. All sentences, inas-
much as they contain these elements, are supposed to be con-
structed in strict accordance with the above rule. But words
are only superficial things, compared with the principal idea
we wish to tell, so, to attract attention we are at liberty to
change the order of our sentences. The world dislikes too
much sameness, therefore, it is proper that we make sentences
our servants in imparting our knowledge for the intrinsic ideas
of words are nothing compared with what causes us to talk.
But whatever order we choose to make the needed impression,
we wish to be understood as only superficially evading the Law
of Syntax you have read.

Rule—In constructing a sentence, the first care must
be to make it complete.

Rule—In arranging the leaning or subordinate members
of a sentence, care must be taken to connect explanatory words.
Compounds and Post Compounds with the words which they
explain.

Rule—Important modifications of a statement should
be mentioned before the statement itself.

Rule—When a sentence contains a number of Adverbs,
(Adverb Compounds or P. Cs), they should be distributed
over the sentence.

Rule—A sentence should have its clauses knit together
by a close logical connection, and its complete sense should be
suspended until its close.

Rule—A sentence should not close abruptly, or end with
an unemphatic Adverb, or any insignificant word, nor with a
postponed Preposition.

Rule—Prefer simple words.

Rule—Avoid circumlocution, or a roundabout way, of
expressing a simple idea.

Rule—Avoid redundancy, or the addition of words
which the sense does not require.

Rule—Avoid tautology, or the repetition of a word in
a different sense.

Rule—Aim at conveying the maximum of thought in
the minimum of words, i. e., aim at giving as much thought
as possible in least number of words necessary. In other words
tell what you wish to tell fully but economize your words.

Rule—Before speaking or writing a sentence .stop a
moment, construct your sentence and then speak or write.

Rule—Never begin to express a sentence without knowing it from end to end.

The Subject comes before the Verb of Predicate, except in the following circumstances:—

(1)   When not being a Question Pronoun it stands in a Question sentence.

(2)   In Conditional Post Compounds without a Conjunction.   For instance, Were I you.

(3)   In exclamatory sentences.   For instance, How great was my surprise!

(4)   When the words *or* or *nor* come before the Verb performing the function of *not*.   For instance, Nor was he far astray.

(5)   When the Verb is preceded by the expletive there, and the Adverbs here, and there.   For instance, There is no doubt.   Here spreads the lovely vale.   There rose the lofty mountain.

(6)   Sometimes the Subject follows the Predicate after words of saying.   For instance, Quoth he.   You better go, said I.

(7)   For the sake of novelty to attract attention, in other words for the sake of emphasis.   For instance, Red as a rose is she.

Rule 2.—The Object follows the Predicate.   For instance, John reads the book.

There are two cases where the evading of this law is proper.

(1)   When the Object is an Introducing Pronoun, a Question Pronoun, or a Noun limited by an Interrogative Adjective.   For instance, That is the tree *that* I felled.   Whom do you see?   Which *waggon* do you prefer?

Rule 3.—The words *a* or *an* and *the* should be used before two or more Nouns following one another when these Nouns denote different objects.   For instance, I saw the Marshall and officer in charge, means that the Marshall was the officer in charge.   But when we mean two persons we ought to say, I saw the Marshall and the officer in charge.

Rule 4.—Introducing Pronouns should be used with some care so that the sentence be easily understood.

It is often well to place the Introducing Pronoun as near to the Antecedent as possible.

Rule 5.—As a rule Prepositions are employed before their objects and are placed as near them as possible.

There are two cases where the Preposition follows its object.

(1) When the object is an Introducing Pronoun or a Question Pronoun.

(2) The Introducing Pronoun *that* should never be used after the Preposition that shows the relationship of action, etc. to it.

(3) The value of emphasis often justifies putting the object ahead in other cases.

Rule 6.—Adjectives precede their Nouns.

Rule 7.—Adjective Compounds and Post Compounds may follow their Nouns.

Rule 8.—Adverbs should be used with precision, that is so as to describe the action, etc. intended.

Rule 9.—Any arrangement of the parts of sentence is proper, if the meaning be plain.

STOPS. POINTS. PAUSES.

Punctuation.

When we speak, we must stop after every statement. spoken, that we may be understood. In penning sentences, signs are used to denote these pauses. In speaking, the tone of the voice and the force aids us in grasping another's meaning. In penning and typesetting, we try to make up for this with signs called punctuation marks. However, in speaking, or reading, we sometimes must stop where there is no mark in order to say two words clearly. But there should be some marks in such places.

The marks are the Period, as John sleeps.

The Question Mark. Who are you?

The Exclamation Mark. Hurrah!

The above are used as a rule after sentences, but the Exclamation Mark may be used after an Interjection.

The Period is used after Declarative and Commanding Sentences. The Question Mark after Question Sentences. The Exclamation Point is used after Wish and Exclamatory Sentences.

Other Marks are the Comma, Semi-colon, Colon, the Dash. ,; : —

A Comma is used to set apart a Compound, as, This morning, he left. A Comma may also be used in setting apart a single word, when such is apt to make our meaning plain. He came, therefore, before dark. The statements forming a Compound Sentence may be divided by Semi-colons. If we want to add a statement to another without writing a separate sentence. we put the Colon between. A departure from the context of our writing is marked by a Dash. Quotation Marks (" ") are used to show that we employ statements exactly as used before.

Synthesis is the making of sentences. It is the converse, or the opposite, of Analysis. It is remarkably more important, because the laws of Etymology and Syntax are *directly* employed towards their object—the correct expression of thought.

[John, London, Halifax, Thursday, June, Flora, Tupper, man, struck, Queen, lamp, little, axe, sun, writes, has, run, new, keen, glorious.]

Supply suitable Individual Nouns and Affecting Verbs in the following sentences:—

———— ———— the table. ———— ———— many people. John ———— the book to me on last ————. ———— ———— a letter.

Supply suitable General Nouns and Unaffecting Verbs, and Adjectives:—

———— ———— mortal. ———— ———— cry. The ————
————that I read ———— on the table. The ———— ———— ————
———— the one I like to chop with. The ———— ———— always welcomed alas, were it never to shine.

[writing, skating, good, strong, well, rapidly, swiftly, sweetly, lovely, driven, written, go.]

Supply suitable Adverbs and Infinitives:—

I am ————, because I like to write. I am skating on the ice. He walks ————. I have ———— rapidly so my horse is tired. He has ———— me back heartily. I shall ———— to-morrow. I have ———— a long letter.

Supply suitable Conjunctions:—

[that, and, but, for, unless, because.]

———— you are learned, he will respect you. It is sad ————he is so ill. I will sue ———— he pays me. John ———— James are well.

[seeing, writing, walking, playing.]

Supply suitable Gerunds:—

Seeing is ————. ———— books is pleasant. He is fond of ————. Children like ————.

[under, on, upon, behind, around.]

Supply suitable Prepositions:—

The book is ————the desk. He lay like a warrior taking his rest, with his martial cloak ———— him. He stood ———— a tree.

driving, teaching.
Supply suitable Affecting Active Adverbs:—
I was ——— a team. I was ——— him.

ADVANCED SYNTHESIS.

Directions.—Write the Subject on a line by itself
" " Verb " "
If the Verb be Affecting, write the Object on a line by
itself.

Write the Adjectives, each on a line by itself.

Write each Adverb, or Adverb Compound, on a line by
itself.

Arrange these parts in accordance with the laws of **Etymology** and **Syntax**.

EXAMPLE.

The prepositions or constituents of a sentence.
- a. The King gained a victory.
  b. The King ruled over England. (Character of Subj.)
  The victory was decisive. (Character of Obj.)
  d. .It was gained over the Scots. (Adv.)
  e. The battle was fought near Dunbar. (Adv.)
  f. Dunbar is on the east coast of Scotland. (Character
of e.)

  g. This took place in 1294.

The Elements.

Subject—The King. (Char.) of England.
Verb—gained.
Object—victory. (Char.) decisive.
Adverb Compounds—1. over the Scots.
2. near Dunbar. (Char.) on the
east coast of Scotland.
3. in 1294.

The sentence: In 1294, the King of England gained a
decisive victory over the Scots, near Dunbar, Scotland.

Exercise.

a. Malcolm was King of Scotland.
b. He was constrained to reitre.
c. He had come too late to support his confederates.

a. I saw the Queen of France.

b. It is now sixteen or seventeen years since I saw her. (Adv. Comp. of time.)

c. She was then the Dauphiness. (Appositive Adj. Com.)

d. I saw her at Versailles. (Adv. Comp. of time.)

a. There was a conspiracy.

b. It consisted of two parts. (Adj. Comp.)

c. Its object was to subvert the government. (Char. of subj.)

d. The conspiracy was discovered.

e. This took place shortly after the accession of James I. (Adv. Com. of time.)

a. Henry VII. was the founder of a dynasty. (Appos. Adj. Com.)

b. That dynasty was the House of Tudor.

c. He died of Consumption.

d. His death took place at Richmond.

e. Richmond was his favorite palace.

f. The event happened on the 25th of April, 1509.

g. He had reigned twenty-three years and eight months.

h. He was then in the 52nd year of his age.

a. The European nations were conquered by the Romans. (Adv. Comp. of manner.)

b. This conquest had first cemented them into a whole. (Char. of "nations.")

c. They had a second bond of union. (Adj. Com.)

d. It was a still firmer bond.

e. They derived it from Christianity. (Adj. Com.)

f. This Christianity was common to them all. (Adj. Com.)

a. Edgar the Atheling sought a retreat in Scotland.

b. He was the Saxon heir to the throne. (Appos. Adj. Com.)

· Warenne had entered Scotland.

a. He had collected an army. (Adv. Com. to a.)

c. It consisted of forty thousand men. (Char of army)

d. He had levied it in the north of England.

e. His advance was unexpected. (Adv. a.)

f. He was defeated by Wallace.

g. The English army suffered severely. (Adv. Com. of manner.)

h. The battle was fought at Cambuskenneth.

i. Cambuskenneth is near Stirling.

SYNTHESIS OF COMPLEX SENTENCES.

A Complex Sentence is a sentence which, besides its principal predicate, has one or more subordinate, or leaning, clauses or Post Compounds.

In working the following exercises this plan may be adopted:—

I. Write down each member of the principal clause (subj. object, etc.) in a line by itself.

II. Write each subordinate clause beside the member ¡n its superior clause to which it relates.

III. Arrange the clauses according to the laws given at pp.— —.

EXAMPLE I.

The Clauses.

A. The more prudent of the crusaders provided themselves with those precious metals.

    1 a1. Who were not sure (att. to Subj.)

a2. That they should be fed from heaven with a shower of quails or manna (subs.)

Name the principal sentences or statements by A, B, c, d, etc.

Let sentences leaning upon A be named a1, a2, a3, etc.; those leaning upon B, b1, b2, b3, etc.

The detailed analysis of Compound Sentences is to be conducted according to the methods described for Simple and Complex sentences.

Compound sentences often assume a contracted form. This occurs whenever an element, common to all the members, is expressed but once. The common element may be subject, predicate, object or extension. For instance, John reads and writes well. John reads well and John writes well.

A sentence is to be considered simple when a simple predicate has for its subject two or more Nouns coupled by *and*.

Sentences may be analyzed as simple, when a simple predicate has two or more objects, or two or more extensions.

2a1. Which in every country are the representatives of every commodity. (Char. of "metals.")

The Elements.

A1. Subject—The more prudent of the crusaders.
Verb—provided.
Object—themselves.
2 Adv. Com.—with those precious metals
1a1. who were not sure a2. that they should be fed from heaven with a shower of quails or manna.
2a1. which in every country are the representatives of every commodity.

The Sentence: The more prudent of the crusaders, who were not sure that they should be fed from heaven with a shower of quails or manna, provided themselves with those precious metals, which in every country are the representatives of every commodity.

EXAMPLE II.

The Prepositions.

A. Tyranny would have ruled without control.
1a1. Tyranny was breaking through all barriers on every favourable moment. (Char. of subj.)
2a1. The nobility had not been free and brave. (Adv. Post Compound of condition.)
a2. The people were poor and disunited. (Adv. Post Compound of time.

The Elements.

Subject—Tyranny
Verb—would
Adverb—have ruled.
Adverb—without control
1a1. which was breaking through all barriers on every favorable moment.
2a1. If the nobility had not been free and brave a2. when the people were poor and disunited.

In accordance with a previous rule we should begin with the clause of condition. At the same time we interweave with it the clause of time which modifies it and the following is the result:—

If, when the people were poor and disunited, the nobility had not been free and brave, that tyranny which was breaking through all barriers on every side, would have ruled without control.

Exercise.

A. History has frequently taught me.

a1. That the head has the very next (day) been fixed upon a pole. (Noun Post Compound.)

a2. Which has one day grown giddy with the roar of a million. (Char. of subj.)

A. The variation of the needle filled the companions of Columbus with terror.

a1. Which is now familiar. (Char. of subj.)

a2. Though it still remains one of the mysteries of nature. (Adv. Post Compound of concession.)

a3. Into the cause of which the sagacity of man hath not been able to penetrate. (Char. of mysteries.)

A. Alexander VI. perceived the townsmen busy in the market place pulling down a figure from a gibbet.

1a1. As he was entering a little town in the neighbourhood of Rome. (Adv. Comp. of time.)

a2. Which had just been evacuated by the enemy. (Char. of "town.")

2a1. Which had been designed to represent himself. (Char. of figure.)

A. These ruling principles are in truth everything and all in all.

a1. Which in the opinion of such men have no substantial existence. (Char. of subj.)

a2. As I have mentioned. (Char. of subj.)

A NOTE ON THE SYNTHESIS OF COMPOUND SENTENCES.

In a Compound Sentence, a principal without subordinate clauses is called a Simple Clause, and a principal clause with subordinate clauses is called a Complex Clause.

The leading divisions or parts of the Compound Sentence are dealt with in the same manner as Simple and Complex Sentences. The only point of difference that remains is the manner of connecting these princiapl members or parts with each or one another. The relation between them is that of co-ordination.

The connectives are usually and, but, or, either, nor, expressed or supposed.

Copulative co-ordination is expressed by *and.*
Alternative   "   "   "   *either, or.*
Antithectical   "   "   '   *but,*
Negative   '   '   *neither, nor.*

EXAMPLE.

a1.   At times industry and the arts flourish.   (Char. of "times.")

A.   In these times men are kept in perpetual occupation.

B.   They enjoy the occupation itself as their reward.

c1.   Some pleasures are the fruits of their labours.   (Char. of obj.)

C.   They also enjoy these pleasures as their reward.

The Leading Members—A.   In times when the arts flourish, men are kept in perpetual occupation.   B.   And they enjoy as their reward the occupation itself.   C.   As well as those pleasures which are the fruits of their labours.

The Compound Sentence—In times when industry and the arts flourish, men are kept in perpetual occupation; and enjoy as their reward the occupation itself, as well as those pleasures which are the fruit of their labour.

A.   I may at least plead in excuse.

1a1.   If I accomplish the present task but imperfectly. (Adv. Comp. condition.)

2a1.   That the present has not been previously attempted. (Noun Post Compound.)

B.   And I therefore request.

b1.   That you will view rather as the outline of reasoning, than as anything pretending to finished arugment.   (Noun Post. Comp.)

b2.   What I have to state on this subject.   (Noun Post Compound obj.)

A.   This might serve to teach the great.

1a1.   If the great could be taught any lesson.   (Adv. P. C. of condition.)

2a1.   Their glory upon how weak a foundation.   (Noun P. C. obj.)

2a2.   Which is built upon popular applause.   (Char. of subj.

B. And they as quickly condemn.

1b1. As such praise. (Adv. Com. man.)

1b2. What seems like merit. (Noun P. C. obj.)

2b1. What has only the appearance of guilt. (Noun P. C. obj.

A. Johnson had seen so much of sharp misery.

B. And Johnson had felt so much sharp misery.

ab. That Johnson was not affected by paltry vexations. (Adv. P. C. of Effect.)

C. And Johnson seemed to think.

c1. That everybody ought to be hardened to these vexations as much.

c2. As Johnson was hardened to these vexations. (Adv. P. C. of Degree.)

a1. We do not discern many stars with our naked eyes. (Char. of stars.)

A. We see many stars by the help of our glasses.

b1. Our telescopes are the finer. (Adv. P. C. degree.)

B. Our discoveries in that proportion are the more. .

ANALYSIS.

When we take anything apart to find out the nature and functions of its parts, we are said to analyze. In grammar, Analysis means a coarse classification of the principal parts of a *sentence.*

A Sentence is a number of words spoken or written that make known a thought. For instance, I worked to-day. But the same words thus arranged do not make a sentence. To-day worked I, because nothing is made known with effect—nothing that adds to the knowledge of anybody.

A Sentence of two words is called a Naked Sentence. For instance, Angus walks. James works. Rain falls.

The Subject of a sentence is made up of the word that stands for what we speak of and other words, etc. used with it, if any, for description. *The good man whom you saw, is going.*

The word that denotes the person or thing spoken of is called the Simple Subject. The red *cow* is in the barn.

Words, etc. employed with the Subject for description, etc. are in Analysis caled En argements. For instance, *That great* man *who is here* was in several battles.

The Predicate is the Verb of a sentence or the Verb combined with other words descriptive of action or state.

The Extension is a name given in Analysis to the Adverb and to any Compound, etc. that discharges the function of an Adverb. For instance, James sang *well*. I came to inquire about him.

There are Extensions of Time, Place, Manner and Cause.

The Extension may be:—

(1)   An Adverb. For instance, John runs *fast*.

(2)   An Adverb, Adjective in form. For instance, Slow he goes on.

(3)   A word which is in form a Noun with or without an attributive. For instance, He stayed an hour.

(4)   Any Adverb Compound. For instance, We live *to learn*. They returned *in great haste*.

THE OBJECT.

The Object is the word in a sentence affected by the action told by an Affecting Verb, together with its words describing it and its Complement, if it have such.

The Simple Object is the word representing the person or thing effected by an Affecting Verb.

The Simple Object often has Enlargements. These Enlargements are either Adjectives in all respects or in function.

Some Affecting Verbs take two Objects.

(1)   These are generally Verbs of calling, naming, choosing, rendering, making, etc. For instance, They made me queen of May. In such cases, the second Object has a complementary force, and is oppositional to the first. It is called the Objective Complement. The Objective Complement may be not only a Noun.

(2)   Verbs of giving, promising, paying, forgiving, etc. are often followed by two Objects. For instance Give John Apples. The first is called the Indirect Object, the second the Direct.

(3)   The Verbs Ask and Teach are often followed by two Objects and both are regarded as Direct.

In the following sentences find the bare or Simple Subject, the Predicate, etc.:—James got a lamp. John is going to Scotland. Travelling is interesting. Sawing wood is good exercise. The old man is tired. A little ship was on the sea. Peters the baker, makes bread. Tom's father was Dick's son. To wait is tiresome. John struck the table. Miss Kennedy plays on the violin. Love one another. They considered him a benefactor. We heard the thunder roll. This news makes me unhappy. . The people made Napoleon First Consul. They chose him as their captain. The teacher gave Charles a long lesson. My father sent me a present. I can procure you a good servant. He killed the bird with a stone. The wind was cold. The beautiful white snow is falling. The King commanded the waves to retire. I write twice a day. May went to Switzerland. May plays on the piano. I bought my daughter a gold watch. I went there by boat long ago. We did term him dishonest. The fire keeps the house warm. He speaks like a child. Of course I shall speak. The timely suggestion was very kindly received. All men who know you call you brother.

A Simple Sentence is one that has one Subject and one Predicate and no more within its bounds. For instance, John saw a bear.

A Complex Sentence is one that contains one independent statement and which has moreover some leaning or dependent statement or statements. For instance, When I came, he went.

A Compound Sentence is one that contains more than one independent statements, each of which may have one or more leaning or Subordinate statements. For instance, When I came in, John left; and after supper, because I was contented, I strolled through the garden.

Subordinate statements are of three classes, Noun, Adjective and Adverbial.

They are called Post Compounds.

Noun Post Compounds are very often introduced by the word *that*. *That*, when so used, is a Subordinating Conjunction.

If a Post Compound performs the function of a Noun, it is a Noun Post-Compound; of an Adverb it is an Adverb Post Compound; of an Adjective it is an Adjective Post Compound.

ANALYSIS OF SIMPLE SENTENCES.

Analysis is either general or detailed.

General Analysis is merely separating the logical subject from the logical predicate, Thus:

Literary life is full of curious Phenomena.

Logical subject, Literary life.

Logical predicate is full of curious phenomena.

Detailed Analysis is naming, so far as they occur in a sentence, the following elements:

1. The subject.
2. Enlargements.
3. Predicate.
4. Object.
5. Enlargements of obj.
6. Objective Complement.
7. Extensions.

Here follow examples of detailed analysis.
The pause in the (1) tournament was still uninterupted.
Subj. the pause.
Enlargement, in the tournament (Adj. Com.)
Predicate, was.
Extensions, 1, uninterrupted, 2, still.

Other geniuses (2) I put in the second class.
Subj. I. Predicate, put. Object, geniuses.
Enlargement of Ob. other, Extension, in the second class.

Her husband, Prince George of Denmark sat in the House as Duke of Cumberland.
Subj. husband, 1, Enl. of subj., her, 2, Prince George of Denmark, Predicate, sat, Extensions 1, as Duke of Cumberland, 2, in the House of Lords.

To attempt to frighten men into morality has never proved successful.
Subject. To attempt to frighten men into morality (Noun Compound), Predicate, has, Object proved (infin.), Extensions 1, never, 2, successful. He seems to have done his duty faithfully. Subject, He, Predicate, seems, Extensions, 1, to have done his duty, 2, faithfully.

ANALYSIS OF COMPLEX SENTENCES.

The general analysis of a complex sentence consists in distinguishing the principal statement from Post Compounds and stating the relation between them. In general analysis, Post Compounds are treated as single words, nouns, adjectives or adverbs. A conjunction connecting a Post Compound with the principal statement is not considered an integral part of the clause which it introduces.
Example of General Analysis of a Complex Sentence:
They said that he would be killed if he attempted that.
Principal Statement, They said.
Post Compounds 1, (that) he would be killed 2, if he attempted that.
Detailed analysis of Complex sentences consists in adding to the above, the analysis of the prin. statement and Post Com. separately.
(1) In detailed represent the prin. statement by the capital A. 2, Represent all Post Com. directly dependent upon the prin. statement by a1, numbering them successfully 1a1, 2a1 3a1, etc. (3) Represent all Post Com. leaning on a1, as 1a2, 2a2, 3a2 etc. Continue this process of notation as far as circumstances may require.

Words necessary to the full grammatical construction are often omitted in the Post Compounds of Complex sentences. For instance, You read better than I (read), I am monarch of all (that) I survey.

EXAMPLES OF ANALYSIS OF COMPLEX SENTENCES.

Whenever he appears in public he is surrounded by his courtiers.

A. He is surrounded by his courtiers.
a1. Whenever he appears in public.

ANALYSIS OF COMPLETE SENTENCE.

Subj.—He. Pred.—is. Extension■—1. Surrounded—2, by his courtiers—3, whenever...in public.

ANALYSIS OF A1,

Subj.—He. Pred.—appears. Extensions—1, whenever.. 2, in public.

2

Those provincials who were permitted to bear arms in the legions were rewarded with a present whose value was continually diminishing.

A. Those provincials were rewarded with a present.
a1. who were permitted to bear arms in the legions.
a2. whose value was continually diminishing.

ANALYSIS OF COMPLETE SENTENCE.

Subj.—Provincials. Enl.—1, those. 2,—who....legions
Predicate—were. Extensions—1, rewarded. 2, with a.. diminishing.

ANALYSIS OF A1.

Subj.—who. Pred.—were. Extension.—permitted to bear ....legions.

NOTE.—In the foregoing sentence the word permitted is a Participle that is a full verb and a full adverb. As a verb it takes to bear for its object. But it is better to regard *permitted to bear....legions* as one extension.

ANALYSIS OF A2.

Subj.—value.
Enl.—whose. Predicate—was.
Extensions.—1 diminishing. 2, continually.

3

What pledge shall I have that you will favour me so kindly as you propose?
A. What pledge shal I have?
a1. (that) you....so kindly.
a2. (as) you propose.
ANALYSIS OF COMPLETE SENTENCE:

Subj.—I. Predicate—shall. Obj.—have.
ANALYSIS OF A1.
Subj.—You. Predicate—will.
Obj.—me. Extensions—so kindly.
ANALYSIS OF A2.
Subj.—You. Predicate.—propose. Ext.—as.

4

Here is a story, which in rough shape, came from a grizzled cripple, whom I saw sunning himself in a waste field alone.
A. Here is á story. a1. which in rougher....a cripple.
a2. whom....alone.
ANALYSIS OF COMPLETE SENTENCE.
Subj.—A story. Enl.—which in rougher....alone.
Predicate.—is. Ext.—here.
ANALYSIS OF AI.
Subj.—which. Predicate.—came. Ext.—1, in rougher shape. 2. from a grizzled cripple.
ANALYSIS OF A2.
Subj.—I. Predicate.—saw. Obj.—whom.
Ext.—1. alone. 2. sunning himself....field.

5

It is a very ancient reproach, suggested by the ignorance or the malice of infidelity that the Christians allured into their party, the most atrocious criminals, who as soon as they were touched by a sense of remorse, were easily persuaded to wash away, in the water of baptism, the guilt of their past conduct, for which the temples of the Gods refused to grant them any expiation.

This sentence is analyzed in tabular form.

Sentence	Kind of Sentence	LOGICAL SUBJ. Bare Subject	LOGICAL SUBJ. Enl.	PREDICATE Verb.	OBJECT Indirect	OBJECT Direct	OBJECT Enl. of Obj.	OBJECT Obj. Com-plement	EXTENSIONS
It is.... expiation	Complete	It	that.... expiation	is					a very ancient reproach suggested ..infidelity.
a1. that the Christians.. criminals	Nun Post Compound	the Christians		allured		crim-inals	most atroc-ious		into their party,
a2. who were easi-ly..con-duct	A. Post Compound enlar. noun criminals	who		were					(1) persuaded to wash away .con-duct. (2) easily.
1a3. As soon as.. remorse	Av. Post Compound modifying Pred. a2	they		were					(1) touched (2) as soon as modifying *touch-ed* by a sense of remorse.
2a3. for which.ex-expiation	Adj. Post Compound	the temples	of the gods	refused		to gra-nt the-m any expia-tion			for which.

ANALYSIS OF COMPOUND SENTENCES.

The principal members of a Compound Sentence are said to be *Co-ordinate.*

There are three kinds of co-ordination. Capulative, Alternative and Antithetcial.

Capulative co-ordination simply joins independent statements. The conjunction *and* usually stands for it, but it is better often to omit *and* for the sake of emphasis.

Sometimes *nor* and *neither* are negative copulas when they are equal to *and not.*

When *who* or *which* has the force of *and* followed by a personal pronoun, it may be considered as copulative and the statement it introduces is not a Post Compound but an independent statement. For instance. The King, who wore a lofty helmet, rode at the head of his army.

Who wore a lofty helmet is employed as a distinction but to give further knowledge. Who is —— to and he that is and followed by a personal pronoun. In such cases who is a Conjunction co-ordinating.

Alternative co-ordination implies the affirmation of one of two statements or the denial of both.

For instance. *Either* you are mistaken or I have lost my memory. He neither ate himself, nor was he willing for others to eat.

Antithetical co-ordination implies a contrast between two sentences. He was not handsome, but he was eloquent.

In analyzing compound sentences the links of connection between the co-ordinate members hould be pointed out.

CPSIA information can be obtained
at www.ICGtesting.com
Printed in the USA
BVHW071442131218
535548BV00018B/676/P